THE LOST TOOLS OF LEARNING

Parson's Porch Books
121 Holly Trail Road, NW
Cleveland, Tennessee 37311

To order additional copies of this book, contact:

Parson's Porch Books
1-423-475-7308
www.parsonsporchbooks.com

Cover photographs: Latin inscribed portico stone from the library at Ephesus by
Eric Killinger. Photograph of Dr. Smith provided by the author.

Cover and book design by Eric Killinger for *Ars Intermundia Expressus*

The Lost Tools of Learning

HOW TO IMPROVE YOUR CHILD'S SAT SCORES

JEFFRY L. SMITH

2011

Parson's Porch Books

Parson's Porch
Books
Cleveland TN

Cleveland, Tennessee

DEDICATION

I would like to dedicate this book to Dorothy L. Sayers, whose writings inspired both the content and the title. Also, to Dr. Jason Ward, Dr. Carrie Wlstead, and Dr. Charles Scalise; and to my editors, Dr. Karen Dolnick and Dr. John Eric Killinger. Thank you all for you support, wisdom, and encouragement.

INTRODUCTION

I N A SPEECH ENTITLED "The Lost Tools of Learning," Dorothy L. Sayers stated, "Even a rudimentary knowledge of Latin cuts down the labor and pains of learning almost any other subject by at least fifty percent" (p. 1).

In my doctoral dissertation (2007), I researched the literature regarding classical Latin, classical Greek, and classical education programs that were utilized in American educational institutions, and their impact on learning in general, and on SAT scores. My purpose was to examine how those classical programs might help ameliorate the current crisis in many public schools where graduating students are not being prepared for college level work—by making learning easier.

The impact of classical studies throughout the history of Western civilization was explored, as well as how even a basic knowledge of classical Latin can ease the work involved in learning almost any other subject. I also wrote about how a return to the methods successfully used for many centuries to educate students would benefit American institutions.

I conducted a qualitative research study using case study methodology, in which data was gathered from teachers of

Latin and/or Greek as well as from students of one or both of those languages. My research demonstrated that classical studies can improve the ability of students to acquire other subjects. With a return to a classical curriculum, Western educators would create an environment for a society composed of educated people who know how to learn, who have the tools to maintain their ability to think freely, and provide a methodology for mastering all subjects.

My experience includes teaching both Latin and Greek at both the secondary and postsecondary levels. I examined Greek as well as Latin because of its similarity to Latin in the form of its declensions and conjugational structure, and since Greek, from which some Latin structures were borrowed, appears to have a similar impact on learning.

Contents

I

MAKING LEARNING EASIER

THIS STUDY EXPLORED THE impact of classical Latin, Greek, and the classical education model on the ability of students to acquire other subjects. Although Latin was the main focus, Greek was dealt with as well. Classical Greek was examined, because of its similarity to classical Latin in the form of its declensions and conjugational structure, since classical Greek, from which some Latin structures were borrowed, appears to have a similar impact on learning.

As Kennedy (2006) points out, for many years Latin teachers have extolled the virtues of Latin as an aid to improving English reading and writing skills, as well as developing thinking and reasoning faculties and, despite the fact that some studies support this contention (e.g., Sheridan, 1976; Masciantonio, 1977), others are less conclusive (Burke, 1985; Haag & Stern, 2003). I have taught both classical Latin and Greek and have also observed this phenomenon.

As Sayers notes, the study of Latin, Greek, and/or a classical curriculum was considered to be of value in the past in easing the difficulty of students in the acquiring of other subjects, and is a "lost tool of learning" (Sayers, 1947: 1) that would be of value in American classrooms. There is a growing perception that education in America is in decline. American students are reportedly falling behind students from other nations. Scholastic Aptitude Test (SAT) scores have fallen. Although American high school graduates are able to matriculate into college, they are unable to write or perform at the college level, resulting in a high rate of attrition during the first year (D'Souza, 1992; Kline 2006; Schmidt, 2007).

The United States Department of Education released a report indicating that "more high school students are taking advanced classes and earning high grades, but they are not doing any better on a federal test aimed at determining how much they have learned" (Schmidt, 2007: 1). The report showed a downward trend in the scores of high school seniors in reading over the last 15 years even though they took "tougher subjects" and GPAs rose "from 2.68 to 2.98" during the same period (p. 1). Some experts posit that this report indicates either that grades have been artificially inflated, or the curriculum for college prep courses have been made easier to accommodate less-prepared students. In contrast, there was a rise from "40% to 68%" among seniors who took "at least the 'standard curriculum,' three credits each of social studies, mathematics, and science, and four credits of English" (p. 1). The same report showed a decline in reading skills from 80% "in 1992 to 73% in 2005" with a corresponding decline in proficiency from "40% to 35%" (p. 1).

Proficiency at high school standard basics was demonstrated by students' recall of college level documents, by "recognizing a sequence of plot elements" (Schmidt, 2007: 1) indicating authors' intent and the motivation of the main characters. Just over half of those graduating superseded the mean scores; about one–fourth demonstrated proficiency, indicating students were not "well-prepared for college" (p. 1). As a further example of the lack of competency in the basics, the New Jersey Education Department's decision to eliminate grammar from the curriculum, as Kline (2006) notes, resulted in ". . . failure rates of 87% in standardized English tests" (p. 1). Many school districts are facing the loss of funding due to failure to meet federal standards, causing many to question the efficacy of the current policy of modern education in American public schools.

This study compared and contrasted current success rates in education with centuries of proven success with Classical Language programs. It elucidated how Latin, in particular, impacted education in the past, can affect the future of education, and how a basic knowledge of classical Latin can ease the difficulty of learning almost any other subject in a significant manner.

By exploring how Latin has impacted education, improved SAT scores, and can be an aid to learning, it has been demonstrated that with a return to the roots of the classical curriculum, educators can create a new environment for society. This society would be composed of educated people who know how to learn, who have the tools to maintain their ability to think freely, and provide a methodology for mastering all subjects.

BACKGROUND OF THE STUDY

Latin is becoming increasingly important as a factor for improving education. The failure rates at the New Jersey School cited by Kline (2006) compared with a successful charter high school in Colorado, which was founded with the promise to parents that their children would be taught a curriculum based on the classical trivium of grammar, logic and rhetoric, provides a contrast between two educational structures. The curriculum includes mandatory completion of Latin 2, and then offers elective courses in Latin 3 and 4—as well as AP college credit courses. The Latin program has proved to be an irresistible draw for parents who value the edge it gives their students in SAT scores. The school has the highest SAT scores in the state, offers AP courses, and has a track record of nearly 100% placement of graduating students in the university of their choice. The waiting list to get into the school has over 4,000 names on it, with slots for only 825 students (TCA, 2007). I taught at The Classical Academy, and witnessed a program that worked well.

The results of the many research studies cited herein indicate that Latin has a positive impact on learning. This information should be shared with those who are in a position to determine curriculum at public schools, and who could support and expand existing Latin programs—namely, the parents and administrators. Further research is required into this phenomenon to determine why Latin students perform so well, and if these results are reproducible or generalizable. Many schools in America are experiencing higher SAT scores and improved learning because of having returned to the lost tools of learning, and Latin in particular. In light of the crisis in the public school system, as evidenced by the devastating results of a shift away from core subjects, the trend needs to be reversed with a return to the proven classical curriculum and Latin. Students are not learning how to learn, are not prepared for college, and, thus, a return to Latin would in effect be a return to higher academic achievement.

As reported in Education Week's *Teacher Magazine* (2007), even older, inner-city public schools can benefit from a Latin program:

Even as educators throughout the country strive after innovative new strategies to improve the literacy skills of low-income and minority students, a small middle school in the Bronx is banking on an old one: teaching Latin. The three-year-old Bronx Latin School is premised on the notion that studying the Classical language, with its intricate grammatical system and building-block vocabulary, will bolster kids' knowledge of English. And there's some evidence to suggest that the plan might be working: On a recent state English exam, Bronx Latin 7th graders outscored their neighborhood peers by nearly 20 percentage points. Skeptics question the long-term practicality of the sometimes-esoteric education initiatives at themed schools like Bronx Latin. But teacher Peter Dodington says that studying Latin is particularly well suited to children who struggle academically. "It's very organized, very transparent," he said. "There's a rule for everything." Plus, learning a dead language long associated with private schools has a way of making students feel special ..." (p. 1).

CLASSICAL LATIN AND THE TRIVIUM

As a Latin teacher, I often used the citation below as a means of demonstrating to parents and students the value of learning Latin. Although this source is sixty years old, it became the underlying basis for this dissertation. There does not appear to be any follow-up in the literature to determine whether in fact this statement is verifiable, and it is believed that this research study will make a contribution toward that gap in the knowledge.

Let me insert here the quote with which I began: "even a rudimentary knowledge of Latin cuts down the labor and pains of learning almost any other subject by at least fifty percent" (p.

1). Dorothy L. Sayers went on to describe the manner in which schools often fail to teach children how to learn, and suggests a return to the language of scholarship and learning used for many centuries, namely, classical Latin. She prefaced that suggestion by another: that "we adopt a suitably modified version of the medieval scholastic curriculum for methodological reasons" (p. 1). Sayers stated that she realized her proposals would almost certainly never be adopted because they are counter to modern thinking and would seem to be turning "back the wheel of progress some four or five hundred years, to the point at which education began to lose sight of its true object, towards the end of the Middle Ages" (p.1). A modified medieval curriculum, she believed, would "produce a society of educated people, fitted to preserve their intellectual freedom amid the complex pressures of our modern society" (p. 1).

Sayers answers the question of why educators would want to "go back" to the Middle Ages with her own question: "Does 'go back' mean a retrogression in time, or the revision of an error?" (p. 1). Her premise is that, if classical education was the model of a truly great education and the current educational model is a watered down, pale copy, a return to those roots would be worth considering today. By returning to the trivium of grammar, dialectic, and rhetoric, students would have a methodology for dealing with any subject.

For many centuries, students were taught Latin, and both lessons and textbooks were exclusively in that language. By learning (a) the grammar or structure of the language; (b) how the language is used; (c) how to accurately define and describe the components; (d) how to construct and detect fallacies in an argument; (e) to embrace logic and dialectic; and finally; (f) by learning to say what they had to say in an eloquent and persuasive manner, students were taught both how to learn and how to defend what they had learned. After mastering these tools, a student would then write a thesis and defend it in front of the faculty, demonstrating mastery in both how to write and how to speak aloud and competently.

In her speech, Sayers (1947) pointed out that Latin is a lost tool of learning. Here is the full quotation:

> I will say at once, quite firmly, that the best grounding for education is the Latin grammar ... simply because even a rudimentary knowledge of Latin cuts down the labour and pains of learning almost any other subject by at least fifty percent. . . . Latin should be begun as early as possible (p. 1).

Sayers (1947) was taught Latin by her mother prior to entering elementary school, and may have been prejudiced or overly enthusiastic about Latin, as indicated by the statement above. If what she says is true, then Latin would be a tremendous tool that modern educators might reassess for aiding in the acquisition of a variety of subjects, and lessening the difficulty of mastering them. Sayers was educated in post–World War II Great Britain, but that model has proved applicable even in current American education settings.

Sayers further stated that most contemporary politicians, authors, editors, pastors, and teachers have never been trained in the classical trivium tradition because the tools of learning have become lost in the maze of diverse curricula, and added:

> The combined folly of a civilization that has forgotten its own roots . . . is forcing [teachers to do] for their pupils the work which the pupils themselves ought to do. For the sole true end of education is simply this: to teach men [sic] how to learn for themselves; and whatever instruction fails to do this is effort spent in vain (p. 1).

Over half a century later, Veith and Kern (2001) corroborated Sayers's original studies when they explored the roots and present use of a Classical education for teachers and parents who were interested in improving the curriculum of their schools or home-schooling their children. The authors believe that in order to "engage in a conversation with the past, the first order of business is to learn the language" of Western culture (p. 21), Latin. The value of Latin is (a) an increased competence in English by learning conjugations and declensions, (b) proficiency in the analytical method and mental gymnastics that strengthen the mind, and (c) putting one directly in touch with the literature at the base of Western Civilization. By neglecting Latin it was argued, culture has been severed from "the stories that constituted its mental infrastructure" (p. 22). The modern return to classical education seeks to remedy the "fatal and arrogant" error of having "jettison(ed) our heritage" (p. 121). It is, however, hard work. Pampered children will be challenged to turn off the TV and read, and teachers will have to convince children that what is good, true, and beautiful has more value than "the glittering prizes of pop culture and the easy answers of relativism" (p. 121).

After all, as Ostler (2007) stated, "[O]nly seen from the perspective of Latin does Europe really show itself as a single story: nothing else was there all the way through ... Latin, properly understood, is something like the soul of Europe's civilization" (p. 2).

The purpose for my writing this book is to explore the educational factors involving the impact of a classical language and/or having a classical education in aiding students to learn other subjects with greater ease than those who have not. I have reviewed the efficacy of studying Latin and/or Greek as a tool for improving all language skills, including composition, improving critical thinking skills, and facilitating learning of other subjects. I investigated the effectiveness of classical studies in supporting greater learning capability and strengthening the cognitive abilities of students, the motivation being the crisis in education today and lack of preparedness by graduating high school students for college or successful careers.

I have described the historical use of Latin in education and the benefits that even a rudimentary knowledge of Latin can have on all grade levels. I have also demonstrated that providing an education in Latin not only improves general English comprehension—including reading, vocabulary, and grammar for both native and non-native speakers—but results in increased verbal and mathematics scores for both the Scholastic Aptitude Test (SAT) and the American College Test (ACT) (DeVane, 1997).

Latin had a long history of favor among the educated hierarchy of early America. As DeVane (1997) notes, Latin is an important "part of the process of developing our children's facility in language usage," and he reminds us that Thomas Jefferson wrote in 1787: "In general, I am of [the] opinion, that till the age of about sixteen, we are best employed on languages: Latin, Greek, French, Spanish" (p. 1).

QUESTIONS WE WILL CONSIDER

1. How and to what extent does a basic knowledge of classical Latin and/or Greek simplify the study of almost any other subject?

2. How and to what extent would a return to a classical curriculum furnish students with the tools necessary for knowing *how* to learn, contribute to their ability to think critically,

and provide a methodology for mastering all subjects?

THE RESEARCH

I chose to use a qualitative research approach that included asking a group of Latin and/or Greek teachers and students who have taken Latin and/or Greek in the past, and adult professionals who have taken Latin and/or Greek a series of open-ended questions. These questions were designed to determine if and the extent to which those who have taken classical Latin and/or Greek have found their intellectual powers heightened, how it impacted how they learn, their understanding of language, their ability to think critically, and "how to defend what they had learned" (Sayers, 1947). I conducted individual interviews, and journals were kept by participants.

The research study examined the perception of former students and current students of classical Latin and Greek in reference to the impact of those languages on their ability to master other subjects. By analyzing the data retrieved from these questions and interviews, I hoped to demonstrate whether those who received training in Latin, Greek, and/or a classical education had found that they were able to learn any subject with greater ease because of these classical tools of education. I asked the teachers involved how and in what ways these tools had impacted the ease of acquiring other subjects—for both them individually, and their students.

SIGNIFICANCE OF THE STUDY

If and when classical language programs are implemented, they will lessen the difficulty in acquiring other subjects, result in higher SAT scores, aid in developing logic, and promote critical thinking. This study was designed to determine if classical language programs will lessen the burden on teachers if students can master their material more quickly. And since material could be covered more quickly, curriculum goals will be reached by the end of the school year, along with the resulting benefits of lowered cost of educating each student. Such benefits would please the school district. All those who have a stake in these issues—including administrators, teachers, and students—would benefit, and also parents, whose children would have more choices of colleges to attend, would be especially gratified.

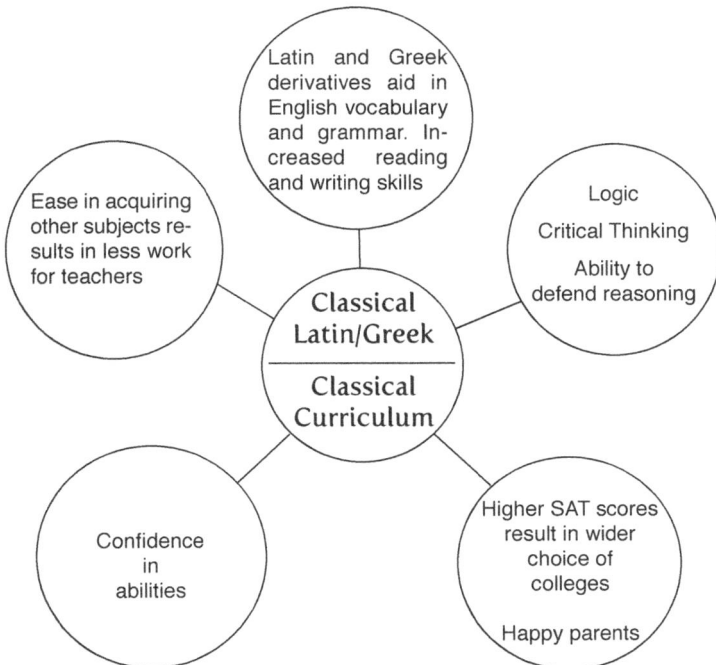

Latin and Greek derivatives aid in English vocabulary and grammar. Increased reading and writing skills

Ease in acquiring other subjects results in less work for teachers

Logic

Critical Thinking

Ability to defend reasoning

Classical Latin/Greek

Classical Curriculum

Confidence in abilities

Higher SAT scores result in wider choice of colleges

Happy parents

DEFINITION OF TERMS

There are only a few terms that will need to be defined to aid those not familiar with linguistics in understanding the terminology. While these definitions are paraphrased, they are based on definitions found in Cook (1993):

> *Critical thinking.* The internalized process of reflective skepticism characterized by identifying, examining, and challenging one's previously trusted assumptions; exploring alternatives; examining context; exploring motives and biases; and scrutinizing what is said or written. However, critical thinking is not characterized by negative or critical attitudes synonymous with being antisocial or belittling.
>
> *Language one (L1).* The first language acquired by an infant.
>
> *Language two (L2).* The second language acquired by humans, either in infancy or as adults.
>
> *Language Acquisition Device (LAD).* The innate ability of human beings to use language that is not learned behavior, and which includes Universal Grammar, a set of rules that are common to all environments where humans acquire languages.
>
> *Primary Language Data (PLD).* The information gathered by children that leads to perception and comprehension of examples of language in use, usually in the form of spoken discourse, which scientists have broken into two categories, comprehensible and comprehended input.
>
> *Quadrivium.* The combination of mathematics, music, astronomy, and geometry, believed since ancient times to comprise a proper education, and to prepare a student to then study the sciences.
>
> *Trivium.* The combination of grammar, logic, and rhetoric in education.

> *Universal Grammar (UG)*. The innate capacity of humans to process LAD with the input of PLD, enabling even a four-year-old to be fluent in one or more languages without coaching or training of any type and without consciously understanding grammar (White, 1989). This innate ability to use language, once developed through the acquisition of the first language (L1), allows a human being to acquire one or more second languages (L2).

There is a need for tools that will provide answers to the current problems in American public schools, and in the field of adult education (Kline, 2006). This study explored whether teaching classical Latin and/or Greek makes learning easier, thinking more critical, and SAT scores significantly higher, and if a classical approach has implications for educators who might wish to take another look at what has worked so well for centuries.

II

A REVIEW OF THE LITERATURE

EDUCATORS HAVE LONG SOUGHT to find a "magic bullet" that will make learning easier. Concepts that have been tried have included Whole Language, self-esteem reinforcement, and a multicultural approach that supplants Western literature with global literature (D'Souza, 1992).

As the church lost its monopoly on teaching and learning, universities advanced, and the classical curriculum was in turn decried and embraced. Although Latin was the language of Western education for many centuries and was an effective tool of learning, it was gradually phased out of more and more curricula (Cohen, 1998).

This chapter explores the literature regarding Latin programs currently in place in American educational institutions, their impact on learning and SAT scores, and the concept of their usefulness for helping to ameliorate the current crisis wherein many public high schools are graduating students who are not prepared for college level work. This chapter also demonstrates how Latin has impacted education in the past, can have a positive influence on the future of education, and how even a basic knowledge of classical Latin can ease the difficulty of learning almost any other subject. By exploring how Latin has impacted education, has improved SAT scores, and can be an aid to learning, it is demonstrated that with a return to our roots in a classical curriculum, educators can create an environment for a society composed of educated people who know how to learn, who have the tools to maintain their ability to think freely, and provide a methodology for mastering all subjects.

This chapter traces key themes in the history of teaching Latin in schools from Roman times to the present, then explores the literature regarding Latin programs currently in place in American educational institutions, their impact on learning and SAT scores, and the concept of their usefulness for helping to ameliorate the crisis wherein many public schools are graduating students unprepared for college level work. The goal is to explore how Latin has impacted education and how a basic knowledge of classical Latin can ease the process of learning almost any other subject.

THEORETICAL FRAMEWORK

In these following chapters, I will be taking a Judeo-Christian view of research, based on Christian andragogy. The roots of that philosophy are found in the Bible, and resemble some of the philosophies extant prior to the information age that purported to explain reality and define how the universe functions (Gutek, 2004). The philosophy stands in antithesis to Postmodernism in that it acknowledges the existence of unchanging values and truths, and a belief in an ultimate reality. I believe that "human reason can discover how the universe, nature, and society function"; empirical scientific methods are "the surest . . . most rational means of finding the truth"; and that science can provide "rational explanations of reality . . . and improve "human life and society" (p. 122).

Christian andragogy seeks to (a) stimulate students to seek knowledge and truth, become lifelong learners, reflectively discerning as they seek to think critically; (b) expose students to all the rich diversity in the world, ethnically and the needs that exist internationally, with sensitivity to all cultures; and (c) provide a quality education through delivery systems that develop professional scholar practitioners who spend a lifetime pursuing professional improvement.

By scrutinizing effectiveness in assessing each student's journey toward competence in communicating in speaking and writing, this philosophy aids students in developing the skills necessary for reasoning, analyzing, interpreting, and integrating knowledge, and teaches competency in researching at the college level. It also seeks to teach students how to demonstrate love and model a sacrificial lifestyle that seeks to serve the poor in actions as well as words as a community in relationship, and to cause the infusion of integrity, respect, concern, and ethical conduct into the personal lives of students in every area: professional, family, academic, and spiritual.

An institution based on the principles of Christian andragogy would have a staff that models attitudes demonstrating to all the members of the community that they are loved, respected, and honored, acknowledging that all forms of discrimination violate the respect due to God's creation. They would seek to integrate the view of truth found in the writings of second and third century Christian philosophers (for example: Justin Martyr, Clement of Alexandria, and Origen) into the curriculum, recognizing that wherever truth is found, it is from God and is grounded in God and in His Word (Hayford, 2001).

Veith (1994) points out that "Deconstructive linguists" hold "that language is intrinsically unstable. Meaning is slippery and changeable; the very meaning-system of our language is clumsy and full of gaps and self-contradictions" (p. 53). This factor would impact any plan for faculty training, in that most of the faculty members in language departments may have been trained to view language as a closed system, rather than an unstable, uncertain one.

One theory of meaning is predicated on the idea that the root meanings of words derive from their antonyms: a man is the opposite of a woman, and a slave is the opposite of a free person. By using the word man, woman is excluded. Each word carries with it what it excludes. Many deconstructionists maintain that meaning is a social construct, and that societies construct meaning through language, and further assume that societies are inherently oppressive. Each group in society, including language groups, must construct their own language, and by doing so, take control over their reality (Veith, 1994).

RELATIONSHIP OF CLASSICAL LANGUAGES
TO MAJOR LITERATURE THEMES

Historical Latin Teaching Methods

In ancient Roman times, education was most often in the hands of a Greek slave, known as a *paedagogus*, who acted as a tutor. Mention is made of this term in Galatians 3:24–25, and in the treatise titled *Paedagogus* (the Instructor) by Clement of Alexandria (c.150–211/216). After five years at a grammar school known as the *ludus litterarius*, children were sent to a grammarian (*grammaticus*) if their parents were wealthy enough. An example of this is influence of the well-known Neo-platonist rhetorician, Libanius of Antioch, who trained both the Cappadocian Father Basil the Great of Caesarea (c. 329/333–379), and early church father, John Chrysostom (347–407) (Gonzalez, 1984).

At the *ludus litterarius*, they studied both Greek and Latin literature. Students read from books that contained no punctuation or spaces between words, had to recite them from memory, and then answer very detailed questions on every word of the books under study.

A typical lesson focusing on a passage from the first line of Book II of Virgil's *Aeneid* is recorded by The Scottish Group (1995) in their Latin textbook, *Ecce Romani*, providing a glimpse into the history of the Latin language and how it was taught in ancient Roman times:

> Teacher: "How many parts of speech are there?"
> Student: "Six."
> Teacher: "How many nouns?"
> Student: "Two. *Omnes* and *ora*."
> Teacher: "How many verbs?"
> Student: "Two. *Conticuere* and *tenebant*."
> Teacher: "What else does it have?"
> Student: "A participle, *intenti*, and a conjunction, *que*."
> Teacher: "What part of speech is *conticuere*?"
> Student: "A verb"
> Teacher: "What tense?"
> Student: "The perfect."
> Teacher: "How is it described?"
> Student: "Indicative, of the second conjugation."
> Teacher: "What voice is it?"
> Student: "Active."
> Teacher: "Tell me the passive" (p. 113).

The lessons continue in this manner for many more questions, each word being treated in the same manner. Lessons taught by rote were drilled ceaselessly into the heads of young Romans. Students who did not master each passage would have their hands or back caned, and if they did not do their homework, they would be sent home to the discipline of their fathers, which could be much more severe.

The History of Classical Latin and the Trivium

Latin developed as an Indo-European language sometime in the sixth century BC, and was the language spoken by inhabitants of the Roman Empire throughout most of Europe and the Mediterranean. When the Western Roman Empire fell around 476 AD, Latin survived in the Romance languages, became the official language of the Roman Catholic Church, and was commonly spoken among the educated classes in Western culture. Declining in popularity in the seventeenth century AD, Latin gradually was assimilated into French, Spanish, Italian, and Romanian, and eventually became part of the English language, which contains some German and French—but as much as 60% of English vocabulary can be traced back to Latin. Ecclesiastical Latin is still used in documents at the Vatican, but not commonly spoken. Latin continues to be taught in many schools in the West, and is very much present in the terms of science, law, medicine, and academic writing. The Latin alphabet is the most widely used alphabet in the world (Latin Language Website, 2007).

The trivium, Lucas (2001) states, with special emphasis on the Greek model of rhetoric, was much admired among ancient Romans as a "useful and honorable study" that many "devoted themselves to . . . both as a means of defense and of acquiring reputation" (p. 25). It was important that an orator had "acquired knowledge of all the sciences and all the great problems of life" (p.25), and Roman education was expected to be pragmatic. An example of this can be seen in Augustine of Hippo (354–430) who was trained as a professor of rhetoric (Gonzalez, 1984).

Latin continued to be the language of literature, education, law, and the church for many centuries until it, as Cohen stated (1998), "began to disappear" (p. 170). Latin thrived in medieval universities as "the exclusive language of instruction" and was "a prerequisite to admission for higher studies" (pp. 47–48). Despite the best efforts of schools such as Oxford, students continued to employ "bad Latin" (p. 49) and many lacked proficiency in the language that was used in teaching and textbooks. Latin and Greek were both popular among the humanists of the Renaissance, due to their interest in returning to the sources of ancient knowledge and wisdom, known as *ad fontes*, "to the founts."

The History of Latin in Education in America

Latin has been important throughout the history of education in America, from the earliest attempts of American institutions to emulate the Latin-based curriculum of England, to a Latin-based school system, and it was the language used in both textbooks and in the classroom. Although Latin waned in popularity in the early twentieth century, it has experienced a recent surge of interest in the last few decades. As Cohen (1998) points out, though students were required to learn, read, and converse in Latin, the depth of their mastery of Latin, even at

Harvard, was shallow in 1680, where students were "hardly able to speak a word of Latin" (p. 24), although this may have had a lot to do with the anti-Catholic tenor of the times. Training in classical Greek and Latin was primarily understood to be especially important to the professions of "law and medicine as well as theology" (p. 29), and vestiges of both languages can still be found in the terminology, phrases, and technical terms of those disciplines today, as well as terms used by all English speaking persons on a daily basis (see APPENDIXES B and C). Greek and Latin were both included in almost every colonial curriculum.

During the emergent nation era (1790–1869), Cohen (1998) wrote, many colleges shifted from a religious to a secular basis, and as a consequence, Latin and Greek, though still considered "proper studies for the educated man" (p. 77) "were falling out of favor" (p. 76) and slowly drifted from core subjects to electives "for those who wanted them" (p. 82). The classical curriculum managed to survive through the emergent nation era due to religious revivalism (p. 81). The Yale Report's 1828 defense of the retention of Latin and Greek was the last attempt to maintain the classical curriculum (Lucas, 1994).

The pragmatic and industrialist 19th century saw further erosion by attacks on classical Latin and Greek as being "languages that are dead ... as far as business affairs are concerned" (Lucas, 1994: 144–145). As modern foreign languages replaced classical ones, controversy arose between the proponents of liberal arts education and those who believed that "modern subjects ... afforded no adequate substitute for the study of Latin and Greek ... and the other elements of the traditional collegiate curriculum" that were proven to "bring your mental powers up to a high degree of efficiency" (Lucas, p. 168).

Entering the University Transformation Era (1870–1944), colleges such as Princeton as late as 1888 were "requiring five books of Caesar and four orations of Cicero" (Lucas, p. 116). Foreign languages were being taught with a view to practical use in "read[ing] literature in the original, supplant[ing] drill in grammar" (Lucas, p. 116). Cohen (1998) states that Latin was losing favor in colleges by the end of the nineteenth century, and yet the statistics provided for 1897, show that "93%" of colleges were still "requiring Latin and 73% Greek" (p. 117). By 1900, Cohen stated, French and German were replacing Latin in college admission requirements for "degree programs in philosophy, letters, and science" (p. 137). High school students taking Latin went from less than 50% in 1910 to fewer than 10% in 1918 (p. 141), and the Classical curriculum continued to decline in popularity from there. In recent decades, however, there has been a dramatic resurgence of interest in Latin because of the ability of Latin to aid in the learning process, while Classical Greek has been less conspicuous, appearing primarily in the curriculums of theological institutions in the form of common or koine Greek, being the original language of the New Testament.

The Basics of Language Acquisition

There is a difference between learning a first language (L1) and learning a second language (L2). Each individual is born with the capacity for using language, but this is not a learned ability. This instinctive knowledge is known as the language acquisition device (LAD), includes the rules of universal grammar (UG), and is found in all humans. Except in cases of developmental limitations, this process begins prior to birth, is most active in children between "eighteen months and six years" of age, and continues at a slightly decelerating pace until shortly after puberty (Gruber-Miller, 2006: 134; Chomsky, 1996).

Basing their patterns of speech on the language (L1) that they hear, during the first year of life, infants learn to how to distinguish between the intonations of words and how to make similar sounds. Sometime before the age of one year, sounds begin to be understood as words, and soon, infants begin to pronounce words themselves. The process of developing syntax begins at around the age of a year and a half; and by the age of three, children "are grammatically correct 90% of the time" (Gruber-Miller, 2006, p. 134). This process requires perception and comprehension of primarily spoken conversations, or primary linguistic data (PLD). The innate components of language acquisition (LAD, UG, and PLD) combined, contribute to the ability of young children to become adept in several languages without requiring any instruction "and without consciously understanding grammar" (Gruber-Miller, 2006: 134; White, 1989).

Once a first language is acquired, these mechanisms allow one or more second languages to be learned. Learning a first language is a unique process that is significantly different from second language acquisition at an older age. As Morrell (2006) stated, although "it is virtually impossible for human beings to develop native accents in a second language after reaching puberty" (p. 135), by exercising their language skills throughout their lives, unless injury or mental illness intervenes, they continue to improve their language skills. These innate mechanisms also allow human beings to acquire languages if enough input is present around them. Fluency in an L2 is an individual trait, resulting in either rapid acquisition for some human beings or slow acquisition in others (Morrell, 2006; Cook, 1993).

There are major differences between learning L1 and L2 (Craig, 2001). The factors that most impact this learning are the age of the student in the process of learning. The first includes the impact of changes in the brain that affect second language acquisition. Plasticity of the brain is lost after puberty, which makes second language acquisition more difficult, but this may be offset by the experience gained by older students that grasp the concepts of grammar, allowing comprehension to overcome physiology. Latin grammar also affects the ability to master the rules of English, and thus improves English comprehension. Another factor is language similarity: if the new language is significantly different (in syntax, grammar, alphabet, and so forth) from the student's L1, the difficulty of acquisition will increase, and the freshman college English grades of Latin students should show improvement (Walqui, 2000; Clark, 2000; Wiley, 1984).

The fact remains, however, that the more input one encounters and comprehends, the faster and more efficient the process of language acquisition. The teaching of a language ultimately represents the process of creating an environment that will allow students to encounter as much input as possible in a way that will engage and facilitate their innate ability to acquire language. This environment can be solely textual, as many curricula are, but ideally the environment will combine textual, visual, and auditory components. The teacher is obviously a crucial component in the environment, but in some courses the teacher's role has generally not been as a source of input but rather of grammatical explication. Consequently, there is a need for curricular materials that can supply the necessary input (Chomsky, 1996). Some postmodernists, who are, according to Gutek (2004), highly suspicious of the "modernist tendency to identify a particular kind of rationality as superior to all others," might see language acquisition from an entirely different perspective.

Finch (2005) described language acquisition as containing

the following concepts: (a) the use of various assessment tools for students that utilize their keeping journals or portfolios rather than traditional testing methods; (b) group work among students in conjunction with self-teaching methods; (c) an eclectic approach that includes many different sources and media; (d) allowing for the expression of indigenous cultures; (e) "deconstruction of propositional language learning concepts" (Finch, 2005: 1); (f) a qualitative approach to group research, and (g) incorporation of an emotion component in language instruction.

Language acquisition also contains a subjective understanding of grammar that rejects "absolute, grammatical 'truths'" (Finch, 2005: 1), moving from a teaching model that is based on the teacher, to one based on the student. Further Finch pointed out that there is (a) an emphasis on both local and international culture in reference to the language being taught; (b) a collaborative approach to tasks; (c) a more free use of the language tools students have learned based upon independent decisions; (d) incorporation of critical thinking skills; and (e) students set their own goals and engage in self-assessment based on individual needs (Finch, 2006). This approach is in keeping with postmodern principles and will "contribute to an effective and meaningful language education" (p. 1).

Johnson, Kritsonis and Herrington (2006) stated that language is "critical for selecting curriculum for the development of the complete person" and that "ordinary human language is the most significant link between curriculum and development of the complete person" (p. 3). Yet, Post-colonialists, suspicious of the "Eurocentric and patriarchal construction of educational theory" (Gutek, 2004: 134), would carefully scrutinize languages such as English, French, German, and Spanish, as having roots in oppressive regimes that regard themselves "as higher and better" than "those subordinate and at the margins of institutions and society" as described in so-called "scientifically objective literature," having components that are actually "racist, classist, and sexist" (Gutek, p. 124). If a language has been loaded with meanings by oppressive regimes such as the French Revolution, the Third Reich, or the Inquisition, those meanings may need to be deconstructed to examine the true meanings behind the root words as understood by the powerless peasantry (Gutek, 2004). Thus, a postmodern language curriculum in a college setting might have to include de-programming language teachers away from the rigid rules and inflexible patterns they had absorbed in their pre-service training (Gutek, 2004).

Since Latin is no longer spoken, nor is it the language of any current regime, political party or power, it is a language that is frozen in time, and can thus presently contains no power dynamics that have been or might be manipulated to oppress or keep a certain ethnic or socio-political group down. The intervening centuries since Rome fell have erased any inherent threat of oppression, and make Latin and/or classical Greek ideal languages for contemporary purposes (Veith & Kern, 2001).

How Latin Aids in Critical Thinking

Much of the literature concerning the benefits of studying Latin is anecdotal, such as (a) the cultural benefits of being exposed to classical literature, considered the basis of Western civilization (Veith & Kern, 2001); (b) learning the building blocks of grammar; and (c) training and exercising the mind in logic, analysis, and deductive reasoning. The following example, however, illustrates the merit of these claims.

Potemra (2002) delineated sixteen steps that are necessary

to accurately translate the Latin sentence, *Vellem mortuuos*, meaning: "I would that they were dead." Although this sentence contains only two words in Latin, to translate it into English one must know: (a) the person (first); (b) the tense (imperfect); (c) the voice (active); (d) the number (singular); (e) the mood of the verb (subjunctive); (f) the root word from which it is derived (*volo*); (g) what *volo* means (I wish); (h) what the subjunctive mood indicates and how to translate it (something urged or wished for); (i) for *mortuuos*: the case (accusative); (j) the number (plural); (k) the gender (masculine); (l) the meaning of the root *mortuus* (dead); (m) the function of the accusative case (indirect statement or infinitive construction); (n) the implied antecedent to the idea of whom the subject wishes were dead that agrees with *mortuuos* (those ones, or those men that are wished to be dead); and (o) because of the indirect statement, there is an infinitive (*esse*, to be) that has been elided, which makes a complete sentence out of what would otherwise make no sense: "I would wish dead."

If any one of these sixteen steps is done incorrectly, the translation will be erroneous. In other words, "In Latin, you must be absolutely right, or you are not right at all" (Potemra, 2002, p. 58). These steps listed above demonstrate the precise logic required by Latin that develops the ability to think critically and analytically.

Additional Benefits of Classical Training

The literature supports the benefits of classical training that comprise the general groupings of (a) aiding in English comprehension; (b) facilitating the acquisition of additional languages; (c) improved SAT scores; and (d) higher grades in

college. As Kennedy (2006) states, improved English comprehension is reflected in higher reading scores (District of Columbia Public Schools, 1971); and in better understanding of
English vocabulary (Masciantonio, 1977). When the District
of Columbia compared the vocabulary and reading skills of over
1,100 sixth-graders who did not receive any foreign language
instruction with a group of Latin students, the Latin students
showed a significant improvement in reading skills. In the study
cited by Masciantonio (1977), over 4,000 elementary students
(fourth, fifth, and sixth-graders) received 15–20 minutes of instruction in Latin each day, and the matched control group
scored a full year lower in English vocabulary.

Another study reported by Kennedy (2006), involved randomly selected seventh-graders who received regular Latin instruction and bested students in the control group by placing
eight months ahead in vocabulary and thirteen months further
in reading comprehension scores. In a group of studies cited by
Ganschow and Sparks (1995) that took place in 1922, 50 Latin
students were compared to 50 non-Latin students that showed
an 18% larger vocabulary and an improvement in writing skills
of 6.5% by the Latin students, and noted that students who had
take a foreign language showed evidence of increased skills in
English. And Van Tassel-Baska (1987) documented "an enhanced reading ability for students who had taken" a mere one
year of Latin, over fourth-year Spanish and French students (p.
16). Other studies, such as that conducted by the Indianapolis
Public School system (Sheridan, 1976) showed similar results,
with a significant additional improvement in math computa-
tion, concepts, and problem solving.

Latin is a natural foundation for improving vocabulary,
since 60–70% of the English vocabulary is derived directly or
indirectly from Latin (California State Board of Education,

2003; Eskenazi, 2000; Ruccolo, 2004). Other studies demonstrating improved vocabulary are: Sparks, Fluharty, Ganschow and Little (1995–1996) and VanTassel-Baska (2004). Abbott (1991), Ganschow and Sparks (1995), and Prager (2000), especially, supported the improved ability of Latin students to learn other languages, with the greatest facility occurring in Romance languages such as Spanish and French, which are based on Latin (Kennedy, 2006).

Devane (1997) has documented that SAT test scores for Latin students with two or more years of Latin have been consistently higher (from 140–160 points) than their peers for several decades. Specifically, in 2003 the National Committee for Latin and Greek noted that students who took the SAT II Latin test averaged "674, compared to the national average of 508" (p. 18). The next highest was French (642), then Hebrew at (630), followed by German (627), and Spanish (575). Classical language students also posted the highest GRE [Graduate Record Examination] verbal scores (as cited by Kennedy, 2006). College GPAs and freshman English grades show a significant improvement (as cited by Wiley 1984, 1989), wherein, of the 44,000 freshmen in the University of Tennessee, Latin students had achieved GPAs of 2.89; French students (2.78), German students (2.77), Spanish (2.76), and those who took no foreign language at all (2.58) (Kennedy, 2006).

Opponents

The following studies noted by Kennedy (2006) indicate that since 1935, there have been opponents to the instruction of Latin in the American school system (Progressive Education Association, 1935). Abbott (1991) stated that Latin was a language that only the most capable students can master, and Paul (2000) believes it is a "dead language and irrelevant" (Kennedy, 2006, p. 20) while Harrington-Leuker, (1992) pronounced Latin to be of "no practical value outside of the classroom" (Kennedy, 2006, p. 20). Burke (1985), followed 51 language students (Latin, Spanish, and French) during three semesters, and concluded that Latin students were no better in English than the other language students. Burke concluded, however, that his study was flawed and that more research was needed, and that small sample size may have been a factor (Kennedy, 2006).

Haag and Stern (2003) compared how well native German speakers were able to learn other languages, but their study was inconclusive. Identifiable gaps in knowledge occur as to whether or not high school Latin students do better in English than students of modern languages. Another gap is in the arena of Latin study and whether or not it extends beyond English proficiency to greater levels of overall student achievement. This study will address those issues. Further, there is a gap in the comparison between: (a) other foreign languages studied and Latin; (b) scores in high school English courses; (c) critical reading scores; (d) writing scores; (e) overall grades; (f) P scores; and (g) in whether having studied Latin impacted "overall academic achievement" over time, and the impact of gender (Kennedy, 2006, p. 23).

RESEARCH STUDIES

The studies below were conducted in order to demonstrate the impact of Latin on both learning and SAT scores, and have provided information about the efficacy of Latin in easing the acquisition of new subjects for Latin students. This information is significant for school districts and all stakeholders such as teachers, students, parents, and the community. Benefits include (a) a lower burden on other teachers if students can master their material more quickly; (b) the lowered cost of educating each student because of that factor; (c) improved SAT scores; (d) satisfaction in learning for students; and (e) higher SAT scores open doors to more colleges, and this is a benefit for parents.

Over the last few decades, Latin has been used in a variety of ways to aid in learning. The following studies show improvement in biology, SAT scores, and English vocabulary. Also, studies have been conducted to explore the way in which Latin is being taught online for schools without the resources to teach Latin, as well as the rationale for teaching Latin. Those studies are examined below, along with the classical education model that is surging in popularity, which model recommends Latin as a lost tool of learning.

In the first study to be examined, De Souza-Wyatt (2002) described the efforts of a teacher to improve learning in her high school biology class through the use of Latin and Greek vocabulary words. The author admits she has no formal methodology and that she tried a combination of eight different approaches at the same time, the method pertinent to this question being: teaching Latin and Greek vocabulary words. She saw her passing rates jump to 83.7%, although she did not relate what the passing rates were prior to her study. Her methods were random and eclectic, but she tried to keep all of the teachers involved in her project up to date via: "e-mail, common planning periods, and after school meetings of what chapters, concepts, vocabulary, etc. were being covered in biology in a given week so that they could provide support to the ESOL [English Speakers of Other Languages] students." She distributed to the teachers "a list of Latin and Greek root words to help with learning vocabulary" (p. 15).

The study indicated that overall biology scores improved. There were no overt recommendations made, only the statement that she felt that a more organized study might show which of the eight methods she tried had the most impact on test scores. The implications of the study are that a correlation might exist between improved scores due to the introduction of Latin and Greek vocabulary to the students. De Souza-Wyatt (2002) believed that she and her teachers and students "all worked very hard throughout the year and that [her] students learned a lot of good biology . . . and also gained insights into how they learn and how they can become better learners" (p. 23).

In her own words, she stated, "The final success of the cumulative effect of this multi-strategy approach is evident in the 87.5% pass rate earned by my students," and further affirmed that she had "maintained (and even slightly improved) the pass rate of (her) students from the previous year." She spoke of "all the qualitative and quantitative data collected" that "give me confidence that the time and effort invested in this approach to learning directly resulted in this outstanding performance by my LEP [Limited English Proficiency] students on the 2002 Biology SOL [Standards of Learning] test" (p. 23).

She stated that she will continue to use this multi-strategy approach during the next school year in preparation for the 2003 Biology SOL exam. As she indicated, the study was subjective, disorganized, unfocused, as well as badly conceived, executed and documented. It was not done in a scientific manner, and used undefined, non-random, convenience samples. DeSouza-Wyatt further informed readers that further studies were needed to corroborate her results, and that an entire new study that only looked at how teaching Latin and Greek derivatives aided students in learning biology terms would be needed to demonstrate whether that method had any impact or not. She further wished that the study had done a more thorough job of explaining the literature that demonstrates this fact by a researcher who uses quantitative and qualitative methods and good documentation.

A second study by Holmes and Keffer (1995) sought to describe how allowing students to use a computer program over a period of six weeks was in teaching:

> . . . high school students to use Latin and Greek root words for deciphering English terms to increase their scores on the verbal portion of the Scholastic Aptitude Test [SAT] . . . Of interest to us in the present study is the question of whether a program of study of Latin terms that is short term can have a significant positive impact upon SAT verbal scores (p. 1).

The design methodology used was a Solomon four-group design, where the researcher randomly assigned students to the following four groups. Group 1 was first given a retired verbal SAT test, then used a computer program (based on the Apple Hypercard system) for two 45-minute periods each week for a period of six weeks. The program taught both Latin and Greek root words as well as how to find those roots in English words, and finally, Group 1, took a different retired verbal SAT test. Group 2 took the same pretest and the same post test. Group 3 had no pretest, but did participate in using the same computer program, followed by the same post test. Group 4 had neither the pretest nor the computer training, but did take the same post test (Holmes & Keffer, 1995).

There were no overt recommendations made, but Holmes and Keffer, (1995) stated that due to the methodology and meta-analysis, they demonstrated that "in some instances rapid improvement in SAT verbal scores, of an order of magnitude approaching .4 standard deviation, may be achieved" (p. 3) by the introduction of Latin and Greek roots into the curriculum. The researchers stated: (a) that their demographics may not be typical; (b) that the only students who participated were volunteers taken from the college-preparatory-level English classes at one high school in northeast Georgia; (c) the high school students are from a "mixed socio-cultural background" composed of about "15% . . . Black," and, that there were economic variables implicit in that 16% of those high school students "received free or reduced-price lunches" (p. 2). The SAT scores of this high school fall well below the national average. But, of the participants in this study, none received free or reduced-price lunches, and only 4 of the 115 volunteers were Black, and thus, the study students were "not representative of the school population as a whole," hence: as "the subjects were volunteers recruited at one northeast Georgia high school . . . generalizability may be limited" (p. 4). Another concern was that, although it was reported that the four groups were composed of males and females, the groupings may have skewed the findings: "Male/female Group 1: 5/10 Group 2: 7/12 Group 3: 10/9 Group 4: 1/16" (p. 2).

Holmes and Keffer (1995), reported that the groups that received the computer training (Groups 1 and 3) were composed of a disparate ratio of males to females, compared to the ratio in Groups 2 and 4. A more even distribution, or a study with segregated genders might show if gender made a significant difference in the results. There was some "significant rises in SAT scores" and "researchers who investigated the effects of the teaching of Latin upon English verbal skills uniformly found a positive effect and disagreed only on the magnitude of the effect" (p. 4). No research was cited directly, however.

Further, although there was not one study cited to document their claim, the authors noted: "A knowledge of Latin and Greek root words has improved the English skills of students through a broad range of grade levels" (p. 4). The researchers then went on to cautiously conclude: "Students of our times are highly motivated to become involved in any activity that has the flavor of a video game. The combination of these two factors may be one approach that can work to improve verbal skills for many students" (p. 4).

This study by Holmes and Keffer, (1995) utilized a pretest/post test 4 group format, and demonstrates a significant improvement in what it set out to show, that knowing Latin and Greek roots can enable students to decipher unfamiliar English vocabulary words. The researchers believed that a more complete and larger study may be needed, which would include an urban high school, and a study that separated the groups by gender.

A third study by Jacobsen (2004) who taught Latin to middle school students at the Shawnee Mission East, used a convenience sample, and she stated that it did not produce usable results. The study was made with the goal of presenting it to the Shawnee Mission Board of Education, which seems to suggest bias may be present, since she started out to prove that Latin would help her students improve performance, as it had in several studies she cites. The study did not include a random sampling, did not produce useable results. Donna V. Jacobsen conducted the study, but there is no listing of her credentials, training or qualifications and there is no information on the Internet or in the study. The only information given is that she is a teacher. The title of the study is general, and it is purported to be one that demonstrated the impact of Latin on the acquisition of English vocabulary and described the effect that teaching Latin had on 27 ninth grade students enrolled in Latin I at an Indian mission school in Arizona. There is no indication that generalizations over a wider population are applicable.

Jacobsen (2004) hypothesized that "ninth grade students who have studied Latin for three quarters of a school year will achieve a higher percentile rank (compared with ninth grade students) on the vocabulary subtest of the ITED (Iowa Tests of Educational Development) than they did in the eighth grade (compared with eighth grade students)" (p. 4). Jacobsen did not do a pretest, but used the previous year's scores from 2003 on the vocabulary section of the ITED test for the 27 students when they were eighth graders and compared it to their scores as ninth graders after they had taken Latin I. Jacobsen summed up her findings in the abstract, "Four students significantly increased their percentile; 23 students maintained their percentile, and none declined. When the grade equivalent scores were examined, approximately half the students showed a grade equivalence increase of 1.5 or greater" (p. 2).

She expressed her reservations in her conclusion, stating that:

> the study raised more questions than it answered. While students did not show significant improvement when their scores were compared to National Percentile rankings, approximately half of the students showed individual improvement according to the grade level equivalents. It's possible that Latin has the most impact on vocabulary development on students whose percentile scores are below 90%. All four of the students who showed improvement were at percentiles of 85 or below. It's also possible that three quarters of Latin is not a long enough time to see significant English vocabulary improvement (p. 7).

She acknowledged that there were other problems:

> One reason for these disappointing results might be the high
> level of achievement the students demonstrated in the eighth
> grade administration of the test. Sixteen of the students had per-
> centile rankings of 92 or higher. (These high levels were not
> known at the time the project was designed.) (p. 7)

Sampling

A potential flaw in the sampling is seen in Jacobsen's statement that "many students who elect Latin already have achieved
too high level for improvement to show" (p.7). If only students
who have chosen to take Latin are used in a study, the results
will be skewed by the fact that those who would choose to take
a classical language may not reflect the average student, and not
reveal how Latin improves all students' SAT scores, for example.

The standard used to determine measurement of change
was: Jacobsen thought that "the ITED does not appear to be a
useful means of measuring vocabulary improvement in Latin
students because many students who elect Latin already have
achieved too high level for improvement to show" (p. 7). "Perhaps greater improvement would be seen after two or three years
of Latin study" (p. 7). Latin did have a positive effect on the test
students. None of the 27 students in the study "showed a statis-
tically-significant decline," meaning that "100% of the Latin students maintained or improved their percentile rankings" for
overall student grades (p. 5).

There did not appear to be any evidence that the author
committed either a Type I error of "rejecting the null hypothesis

when it is true" or a "Type II error ... by accepting the null hypothesis when it is false" (Sytsma, 2006). Neither was there evidence that she had actively sought to engage in theoretical sampling, which, "in qualitative studies" consists of selecting "study participants based on emerging findings to ensure adequate representation of important themes" (Sytsma, 2006). In the description of the population, it was indicated that subjects were chosen randomly, had great divergence in background, gender, level of education, age, jobs, and so forth, allowing a greater probability that differences will emerge clearly and that results can be generalized, resulting in a convenience sample.

The final paragraph by Jacobsen (2004: 7) stated:

> The results of this study are inconclusive, but further research might help determine more precisely how Latin study improves student performance with the English language ... Perhaps student progress could be more accurately measured by means other than percentile rank ... Almost everyone who has studied Latin anecdotally attests to the enormous impact it has had on English vocabulary. It is worthwhile to develop more studies to learn how twenty-first century students can best benefit from this ancient, vital language.

A fourth paper by Jordan (1999) addressed the advantages and benefits for those students who had taken Latin in reference to their SAT scores, versus those in other language groups. She stated that there were "incontrovertible figures that administrators and parents should know if Latin teachers are going to convince them of the benefits that students receive from studying Latin." Jordan (2001: 1) provides the averaged SAT scores of students who took Latin in comparison with all students, and with those who took Spanish, French and German: (a) All students, 505; (b) Latin, 662; (c) Spanish, 590; (d) French: 632;

and (e) German, 623.

The author of the study believed that these findings demonstrated that overall SAT scores were much higher among Latin students than among students who had taken other languages in this particular instance. Although Latin students performed better on SAT tests, the academic profile of these students before they took Latin was not noted. Although the previous studies indicate that Latin students performed better SAT tests, there were factors not considered. They are: (a) the possibility that smarter students are drawn to take Latin rather than other languages; (b) whether confidence in one's scholastic abilities gives some students the confidence to take a subject such as Latin; (c) the fact that Latin is generally taught at schools that would have higher SAT scores anyway; (d) the influence of resentment in schools where Latin is a required subject; (e) the significance of taking higher levels of Latin (III, IV and AP) on SAT scores compared to those who stop at the lower levels of Latin; and (f) the impact of affluence on performance.

A fifth study was conducted by Shelton (2000) who, at the time of the study, had nineteen years of experience in teaching Latin, and recently began teaching Latin online. She stated that it was a great alternative way to learn Latin, and may be the only way some students can find to study Latin, due to the lack of availability in many brick and mortar schools.

In-service training was given to traditional teachers, and they began their teaching with a phone call to each student; the lessons were broken down by weekly requirements; students made contact weekly with the instructor; there was phone contact and e-mail messaging between both teachers and students and between the students themselves. The teaching of Latin has come full circle from strict rote memorization and grilling to the use of modern technology. Shelton (2000) describes her experiences in teaching Latin online but offers no conclusions or results.

A sixth study by Baumler (1980) describes how Latin has made a comeback in America and cites a study in Philadelphia, which showed "significant improvement in vocabulary and reading ability in English" (p. 1). It points out that even though elementary school age children can acquire another language with great facility, less than 1% of them are receiving any instruction in foreign languages. Although half of all high school students take Latin at the start of the 20th century, only 1% do so today, taking also into account that both the number and the percentage of high school students now is much higher than in 1900. Yet studies indicate that Latin students "receive higher scores on their College Entrance Exams, and have better English grades and vocabularies" (p. 1).

Because Latin works differently than English, it provides a means of not only improved knowledge of grammar and syntax, but is helpful in learning other languages. Baumler (1980) concludes: "Education that neglects the past is unthinkable, suicidal," and Latin "enables one to live intellectually in the distant past out of which all Western cultures developed." And further, Latin "enlarges the pupil's mental horizon by introducing him to a completely new medium of verbal expression and communication and cultural pattern" (p. 1).

Classical Education in the 21st Century

In their book on classical education, Veith and Kern (2001) explain the roots and present use of a classical education for educators and parents interested in changing the curriculum of their schools, or in home-schooling their children. The authors believe a classical education "cultivates wisdom and virtue" and that it is based on "truth, goodness and beauty" (p. 11). They point out that a classical education is based on the liberal arts curriculum, and that by "liberal" they intend its basic Latin meaning, derived from *libera*, meaning freedom (p. 11).

By studying the liberal arts, all human faculties are engaged: the trivium of grammar, logic, and rhetoric; and the quadrivium of mathematics, music, astronomy, and geometry, once mastered, prepare a student to then study the sciences: "natural science (which included both the physical and the metaphysical), moral science (which contained history, politics, and law), and theological science (the study of religion and first principles)" (Veith & Kern (2001: 11). Following this preparation, a student is then prepared for professional studies in "law, medicine, or the church" (p. 11).

Conspicuously absent are such subjects as literature, art, psychology, computer science, and the like, yet they also have their place in a classical curriculum. Literature would fall under the heading of grammar, and psychology is a moral science, and so forth. The trivium and quadrivium, the authors believe, are not subjects, but modes of learning (Veith & Kern, 2001: 12). The authors are not in favor of that kind of "critical thinking" that is in reality "an applied skepticism," resulting not in formal logic or lessons in common sense, but the questioning of "moral authorities and [the] undermin[ing of] traditional values" (p. 14).

Quantitative Comparison of Latin students

The following data was gleaned from a research study conducted by Kennedy (2006):

> In comparison with students who studied a modern foreign lan-
> guage, students who studied Latin demonstrated higher levels
> of achievement in: (a) English course grades (p. 39) . . . (b) with
> respect to PSAT Critical Reading scores (p. 41) . . . (c) with re-
> spect to PSAT Writing scores (p. 42) . . . (d) with respect to SAT
> Verbal scores (p. 44) . . .with respect to overall GPA scores . . .
> corroborating research noted previously by Sheridan (1976) at
> the elementary level and by Wiley (1984; 1989) at the college
> level (p. 46) . . . with respect to overall PSAT (and SAT) scores
> (p. 48).

Kennedy (2006) concluded that "students who studied
Latin positively differed from students who studied a modern
foreign language with respect to patterns of English achievement during their freshman, sophomore and junior years" (p.
53), "and in patterns of overall academic achievement gains during their freshman, sophomore junior years" (p. 56). "Latin students in the study achieved SAT Math scores 53 points higher
on average than French students and 62 points higher than
Spanish students" (p. 61); and finally, mean scores were as follows: "Latin 598.10; Spanish 535.85; French 544.91" (p. 61).

Differences in Teaching College Level Students Vs. High School Students

As reported by the American Classical League (2007),
there are differences in how high school students learn Latin,
and how college students learn Latin. Each must have "textbooks suited their interests and needs" (p. 149). Because of their
"greater maturity and partly because of their increased capacity

for analytical thinking which they have been busily developing in their other college level classes" college students can "appreciate the complex issues raised by an author such as Cicero . . . even when their Latin skills may still be at a rudimentary level" (p. 149).

Because Latin is more difficult than Spanish, French, or German and has the added disadvantage of not being currently spoken in any country of the world (a quality which some people refer to as being "dead"), many students who are not classics majors still choose to study Latin, despite the fact that it is difficult, impractical, and will not help them in their majors.

The author further states that, "My students tell me that they welcome the intellectual rigor that their study of Latin provides. They say that in the course of studying Latin, their knowledge of English grammar and even their writing style has been greatly enhanced" (p. 149). And in an echo of comments by participants in CHAPTER 4 below, they find great satisfaction in reading deep, complex writers "such as Cicero, in the original Latin, and in being able to understand those authors in their historical context" (p. 149, ACL Newsletter).

CONCLUSION

Several studies have been explored above that examine the role of Latin in aiding learning. The one conducted by De Souza-Wyatt, (2002), described the author's efforts to improve learning in her high school biology class by teaching them Latin and Greek vocabulary words, and saw improved test scores and passing rates of 83.7%. Another that was examined, by Holmes and Keffer (1995), looked at the effectiveness of using a computer program to teach high school students how to use Latin and Greek root words for deciphering English terms and to increase their scores on the verbal portion of the Scholastic Aptitude Test (SAT). As described above, the mean score for participants who received the Latin and Greek training was approximately 40 points higher than the mean of the control groups. The third study presented (Jordan, 2001) showed the various levels of SAT scores achieved by students who took Latin versus those who took Spanish, German, and French. That study indicated Latin to be a more significant factor in higher SAT scores than the other languages and indicated that these findings should be shared with both parents and administrators, and all those who were in a position to support and expand the Latin program.

As educational resources are always scarce, if information from this study was used to guide the apportionment of funds for language education, it might significantly lower the overall cost of education, since it improves both English and math scores, and "would seem to justify current Latin programs . . . especially where needed to assist those students who do poorly in English and math" (Kennedy, 2006: 75). Further research needs to be conducted in this field to determine whether or not causality can be proven, so that stakeholders would be able to justify expending a larger portion of available funds to ensure that Latin is part of the curriculum offered at all schools to boost academic achievement and raise standardized test scores. The following chapter explores the experiences of students, teachers, and former students now pursuing careers to determine why many schools in America are experiencing higher SAT scores and improved learning due to the return of the lost tools of learning.

III

HOW THE STUDY
WAS CONDUCTED

I COLLECTED DATA BY CONDUCTING unstructured individual interviews with both Latin and/or Greek teachers and with students who are currently or who have formerly studied either Latin and/or Greek. I also wrote an ongoing journal describing the contrast between the perceptions of two groups: teachers and students, wherein I compared and contrasted the data in an attempt to understand and analyze participants' perceptions and experience with Latin and/or Greek as a facilitator of learning. By these data collection means, I sought to discover the perception of teachers, students, and professionals regarding the efficacy of Latin as a means of acquiring subjects more easily.

THE PROBLEM I ADDRESSED

"It is not known if and to what extent the study of classical Latin and/or Greek will simplify the study of any other academic subject" leads to the following research questions that were addressed:

1. How and to what extent does a basic knowledge of classical Latin and/or Greek simplify the study of any other subject?

2. How and to what extent would a return to a classical curriculum furnish students with the tools necessary for knowing how to learn, contribute to their ability to think critically, and provide a methodology for mastering all subjects?

My purpose was to contribute to an understanding how to improve the ability of adults to acquire a variety of subjects and to improve the level of education in American public schools.

For the study sample I chose faculty, students and former students who have had recent experience either studying or teaching Latin. By interviewing participants by means of individual interviews consisting of students and instructors, conversations were observed and recorded that generate thoughts regarding the impact of Latin.

I examined the perception of former students and current students of classical Latin and/or Greek in reference to the impact of those languages on their ability to master other subjects. The population that was studied is a sampling of graduate students, students from several universities, and professionals who have taken Latin and/or Greek recently. The sample group consisted of sixteen men and women, ages 20–65. To select the sample, letters were sent and phone calls were made to educators and students known to me, as well as members listed in the current roster of the State Classics Association in my state of Colorado. All those willing to be part of the interview process were included in the study. All those who expressed an interest in the topic were considered for participation.

THE QUESTIONS

1. Which classical language have you taken (Latin or Greek)?
2. What was the level of Latin taken/taught (Beginning Latin or Advanced Latin)?
3. What was the level of Greek taken/taught (Beginning Greek or Advanced Greek)?
4. Do you think that having taken a classical language has impacted your ability to learn other subjects?
5. If yes, which subjects, and in what ways?

All the data was compiled from those who replied to the questions, and the statistics were collected and placed into chart. Results and analysis are shown in TABLE 1 below.

Latin Beginning	Latin Advanced	Greek Beginning	Greek Advanced
2	9	3	5
Positive: ⅔ = 66%	7/9 = 78%	¾ = 75%	5/6 = 83%
Answered "yes" = 76%			
Negative: ⅓ = 33%	2/9 = 22%	¼ = 25%	1/6 = 17%
Answered "no" = 24%			

The consensus of the comments on the questions, interviews and conversations I had with individuals who have taken a classical language were analyzed and are set forth in narrative form in CHAPTER 4.

The interviews began with one broad question: "Did you notice any change in your students' quiz/test scores in other subjects after they took Latin?" Then, the audiotapes that were collected were carefully transcribed verbatim to ensure accurate transcription.

I also requested from each participant in the study, samples of materials related to Latin/Greek and classical education, and are to be found in the APPENDIXES.

As previously stated, the population to be studied was a sampling of sixteen college students from several universities, and teachers who have studied or taught Latin and/or Greek. Confidentiality was preserved in my research study by substituting pseudonyms for the actual names of all participants, which were assigned alphabetically; for example, Mr. A, Ms. B, etc.

IV

WHAT DID THE STUDY SHOW US?

BACKGROUND

WITHOUT EXCEPTION, PARTICIPANTS BELIEVED that there was great benefit in learning a classical language, although they differed in how and why it should be taught. The sixteen participants in this study were seven female and seven male individuals, ages 20 to 65, who currently teach or previously taught either Latin or Greek or both in secondary, college, and postgraduate institutions, and two male individuals who studied Latin and/or Greek at the college level. All interviews were conducted in October, 2007, in person or on the telephone. All journals were also collected in October, 2007. All actual names of participants have been replaced in this research study with pseudonyms to ensure confidentiality.

The interviews lasted from thirty minutes to ninety minutes, and some transcripts ran to over 2,300 words in length, with journals being from four to twelve paragraphs.

I sent out over one hundred letters and e-mails to addresses gleaned from sources such as the Colorado State Classical Association, The American Classical League, and various Latin and Greek teachers Web sites. From those, ten agreed to participate. The remaining six were teachers and students known to me personally. The interviews were relaxed and conversational. The interviewees shared with me that they had spent time reflecting on the topics that had been provided to them prior to the actual interview, and several had written down their thoughts on other related topics they wished to discuss. An attempt was made in each case to allow participants the freedom to discuss these topics as they wished.

The participants encompassed a wide range of experience and expertise, having from five years experience home schooling in one case, to twenty-five years experience in teaching both Greek and Latin in another. Of the sixteen, four were retired, and the remainder currently teaching. Two had published articles in refereed journals, had written books, and had spoken at dozens of conferences on the subject of Latin and Greek. Five have chaired departments, presided over professional organizations, hosted Web sites, and received numerous awards for exemplary teaching.

A variety of teaching experience was found among participants. Four had taught at the college level; the remainder, at the secondary level. Most had been or were currently full time teachers. Participants were located in the following states: six were from Mountain States, three from the West Coast, four from the Midwest, and the remaining three from the East Coast.

The data findings reported in this chapter are based on my analysis of the following data sources: (a) unstructured interviews, (b) journals written by participants, (c) journals and field notes written by me, and (d) artifacts consisting of documents collected from participants.

I designed the following narrative to present both my thoughts and the thoughts of the participants, in a manner that faithfully represents the thinking of both. The sixteen participants provided information regarding their educational and professional backgrounds, interests, and teaching philosophies. All names have been changed to ensure their anonymity. All voices are heard to the extent they participated in interviews and journals, and any items that were extraneous to this research study were omitted. Each participant was allowed to speak freely and I kept prods and probes to a minimum in the interviews, and journals contain none. As a result, varying amounts of data were collected from individual participants, depending on their interest or lack of interest in particular topics, and thus their voices will be heard more often in some sections than others.

Similarities in Latin and Greek

Before proceeding to the data, it is important to clarify the similarities between Latin and Greek as to their impact on learning other subjects. The five participants who had studied both, believed that: The two languages are very similar in terms of discipline, and that Greek grammar and Latin grammar are very alike. Latin grammar tends to be a little more complicated since "Latin is an older language and has had a long time to be pared down to basics," as Ms. King, who has taught both, put it. "And so for that reason, I think the discipline one learns in taking Latin and Greek is very similar. There is a lot of memory work involved, and that improves your memory as you do it."

Ms. King continued:

Both Latin and Greek are aids to learning, and aids to logic—
Latin more than Greek—in the sense that word order in Latin
translation tends to be more complicated. Latin has more dependent clauses that need to be incorporated into the whole.
Greek more or less flows in many of the same ways that modern
languages flow, without the learner having to think of verbs and
of clauses or sentences. Participants agreed that the educational
benefit—just talking about the language itself—is great, but
there are also many cultural advantages.

Categories

The interviews and journals ended up being divided into
quite different categories than the original questions intended.
Recurring themes occurred as represented by the following six
categories:

1. The benefits to studying Latin and/or Greek that
   have been observed by participants in their students
   and in their own education.
2. The impact of studying Latin and/or Greek on understanding and using English.
3. The impact of studying Latin and/or Greek on acquiring other subjects such as math, science, history, culture, and other languages.
4. Reasons that a classical education curriculum is
   rarely taught.
5. Differences in the impact of Latin versus Greek, in
   ease of acquiring other subjects.
6. Problems that exist but would not change if public
   schools decided to switch to a classical curriculum
   or even just to offer Latin and/or Greek.

The process of data collection and the method of presenting data analysis were systematic, and used several different sources in order to fully encompass the research questions in depth. As Bogdan and Biklen (2003) suggest, interviews, journals, and artifacts were collected and analyzed. The research statement that formed the basis for this study was "It is not known if and to what extent the study of classical Latin and/or Greek will simplify the study of any other academic subject." This study had the following two research questions: (1) How and to what extent does a basic knowledge of classical Latin and/or Greek simplify the study of almost any other subject? and (2) how and to what extent would a return to a classical curriculum furnish students with the tools necessary for knowing *how* to learn, contribute to their ability to think critically, and provide a methodology for mastering all subjects?

The focuses of the data gathered was to provide a basis for analyzing the perspectives of various individuals who had taken a classical language; to provide information that I could reflect upon and write about in a journal; and to fully address the research questions. The data analysis technique was composed of both open and selective coding. The first step in analysis was open coding, consisting of an initial identification of themes and categories, but did not include cross-analysis. The constant comparative approach (Bogdan & Biklen, 2003) was used, and data was sifted for new categories until saturation was achieved.

As subcategories were identified, they were sorted according to whether they were positive or negative in perspective. Next, the following sorting took place: (a) interrelationships of categories; (b) phenomenological analysis; (c) expanding on the ways in which various categories built upon or were dependent on each other; and, (d) sorting categories according to their impact on learning.

After the sorting phase, data analysis was begun. Selective coding ensued, with a view to creating a matrix of the thoughts, experiences, feelings, and conclusions reached by both the participants and by me as they related to the underlying theoretical framework.

What follows will be divided into two sections, each section dealing with each of the two research questions, ending with a summary of the findings of the research study.

RESEARCH QUESTION I

The first research question addressed the impact of a basic knowledge of classical Latin and/or Greek on simplifying the study of almost any other subject, and was primarily answered by Latin/Greek teachers, former teachers, former students, and by me.

Interviews were conducted and journals were collected, in which the participants addressed the following:

1. Did you notice any change in your students' quiz/test scores in other subjects after they took Latin?
2. Describe any changes in your ability to understand other subjects since studying Latin.
3. Tell about the ways that knowing Latin has impacted your education, ability to reason logically, and how it has impacted your lifelong learning.

Even though the findings for each of these themes are reported separately, they are interrelated. Where possible, these interactions are described in order to help the reader gain a better understanding of how classical languages impact learning.

Impacts of Classical Languages on Learning

Although one of the purposes for carrying out this study was to gain an understanding of how adult educators perceive the impact of classical languages, during the interviews, participants spoke about overarching goals for the field of adult education. This may have occurred because the initial questions were so open-ended that participants responded by discussing their views of the goals of education in general. However much they differed in perspective, they agreed on many points. From their responses, three broad categories were identified: how classical languages have had a positive effect on their personal lifelong learning; the impact on their students' achievement; and the manner in which their understanding of English has been improved. These three categories are described in the following section. The first theme to emerge from the study was a positive effect upon learning in general from having studied a classical language.

Positive Effects of Classical Languages

Twelve out of the sixteen participants agreed that classical languages have impacted their lives and the lives of their students in a positive manner. The remaining four were reluctant to agree without qualifications, but neither were their comments negations of that premise.

Dr. Adams, a Greek teacher in a seminary, stated how Greek had impacted his learning:

> Being able to read more carefully, just the exercise of learning
> another language helps in your ability to memorize and figuring

out how (one is) going to learn the topic and new subject matter. I think it pays off in a lot of different areas... there are a lot of examples: When translating long sentences, you have to supply various verbs to make sense of what's taking place. Greek is helpful for exercising the mind, and forcing you to think and supply something that isn't there.

Mr. Baker, the most verbose participant, who studied Greek in seminary last year, agreed that Greek was very helpful:

In being able to process reading of different books that have nothing to do with the study of those languages I was able to comprehend subjects, no matter what they are, and actually, in most cases, read more quickly, and comprehend more. To be able to understand the subtle nuances of things and to find out the meaning. To be able to think intelligently about it, instead of just saying something that somebody else has said. When you are able to read the original language itself, it just means more: there's just something more substantial to it. I now have a means of assessing the overarching subject or integrative idea that draws all the subjects together in the education system. This helps a student to understand how they all intertwine with the whole of life and work, or whatever. Latin and Greek are cohesive subjects—a catalyst for understanding. They expand your mind, your thinking abilities.

Another participant, Mr. Charles, a doctoral candidate that I met in Seminary Greek class, stated that:

Greek aids in any sort of learning. It helps you to think beyond your own idioms and cultural expressions. It gives you a broader frame of reference for teaching, for learning, and for life. It helps students with what they communicate in an increasingly globalized world. Engaging with non-Western culture is very important. Realizing that everyone does not speak like Americans.

A Latin teacher, Mr. David, found that "over the years I have had several opportunities to talk with some of my former Latin students and they have all said they were happy to have taken Latin. Also, the study of Latin laid the foundation for my endeavors in the other fields."

Ms. Edwards, a twenty-year veteran teacher of Latin and Greek, posited a reason she believes explains the positive effect of Latin: "When students take Latin, which is considered a difficult language, and they are successful, the transfer to other subjects is in the area of confidence. Thus, I would say, 'Yes,' they do better in other subjects."

A Latin teacher from the East Coast, Mr. Frank, saw a dual benefit to Latin:

> My ability to understand other subjects as a result of studying Latin is both linguistic and substantive. Linguistically, Latin has helped me tremendously in my knowledge of English, but, substantively, the elegance and structure of the language itself has informed my prose style as well.

Mr. Henry, head of the classics department at a large university described his observations regarding his personal experience, and that of his students:

> Latin definitely helps me as a learner. Learning Latin, because it is a schematic language and because it involves an analytical approach and requires a large amount of memorization is good for exercising your brain, and it does lead to improved performance. All my students who are classics majors have had either Latin or Greek in general, and they perform better in my large lecture classes where there are classic majors and non-classics majors intermingled. They are very good students relative to their peers, and one quantitative measure of that is that in the last five years or so, the per capita number of classics majors who

receive honors upon graduation, is the highest in the college of arts and sciences: somewhere in the 20 to 30% range for people graduating with honors. And that outpaces every other department in the university and has for several years.

Ms. Ida, although she teaches Latin to seventh graders and not college students, also noted a similar effect of Latin:

> There is a decisive difference between the students who have been in the program for even one year and new incoming students, in regard to their other classes. After even the first quarter, these new students show noticeable improvement in other classes, especially in English. As the students continue their studies in Latin, their discipline and understanding of language increases. Often their test and quiz scores improve at a similar pace, though how much of this is due to Latin study, and how much is due to excellent discipline and instruction in other courses is impossible to tell.

And she adds on a personal note:

> My reading comprehension in nearly every subject has significantly improved. Latin has impacted my general education in several ways. The discipline required in learning any foreign language inevitably improves self-discipline in other areas. My ability to reason logically has changed dramatically as well.

Other participants who commented on beneficial impacts of classical languages included Ms. John, who taught both Greek and Latin for over twenty years, and thought that:

> The benefit for persons in both reading and writing is tremendous. In reading you understand far better what the words mean. For writing, you have a better understanding of basic grammar and know how the words you're using are actually working in a sentence. Thought processes in learning Latin tend

to be a lot like thought processes in any logical approach, such as to math, for example.

The students of Ms. Lewis, she states:

> Unanimously assert that their Latin study helps them in other subjects, particularly other languages. One student says she never really understood English until she studied Latin, and many students support the often heard refrain that they don't teach English grammar in school any more but encounter this kind of knowledge for the first time while studying a foreign language and especially Latin. I consider Latin indispensable, to the point that I find it hard to consider anyone educated unless they have studied it. For any person who has scholarly aspirations it really is the sine qua non of academic endeavors, not just for the language but for the historical background. Not having a Latin background just puts one at an enormous disadvantage. It is like tying one hand behind your back. It is such a handicap. I can report that several of my students who have gone on to study classics or history are doing very well.

A mother who homeschooled her two children, Ms. Mary, reported a success story:

> In my children's junior and senior year of home-based education, they were able to test into the college level, and achieved up to twenty and thirty college credit hours before they even graduated from high school. They scored high on their SAT scores and were able to get full scholarships to [participant's] State University.

Another Latin teacher in the public school system in the Midwest, Ms. Nancy, had very definite ideas about the value of Latin, if taught properly:

If it is taught as a language and not a programming code, a wide variety of learners with different abilities will succeed at Latin, NOT [sic] just the ones who are detail-oriented. Do I think the chaotic mind might benefit from the logic of the inflectional language? Perhaps. It depends on how it is taught.

Mr. Otis discussed how Latin helped students learn other subjects, as well as critical thinking:

Apparently in middle school they had never had to memorize ANYTHING [sic], and when they took Latin, they figured out how to do that. Not only are they learning and using Latin, but they are acquiring learning skills that serve them well in other areas. I have definitely added things to my repertoire that I did not as a younger teacher—giving them things that are going to help them in their futures as non-Latin speaking adults—making sure they know most of the common Latin expressions used in English (*quid pro quo, et al., etc.*), learning how to watch a "classical" movie with a critical eye, asking questions such as, "How has mythology or history been warped to produce this movie? Why?" And hopefully, to instill a love of those things ancient which have helped make the modern world operate as it does today.

A second theme that emerged during data analysis was the impact of classical language study on English comprehension, grammar, vocabulary, and style. In this section, those findings are presented. The influences that helped bring participants to their understanding of this phenomenon have been woven into the discussion.

Classical Languages as an Aid to Proficiency in English

Dr. Adams, the seminary teacher, believed that "Greek really helps with understanding construction and sentences, since English emphasizes word order," adding the additional comment that studying Greek, "really helps to see that modern translations [of the New Testament] are actually interpretations."

Mr. Baker admitted that prior to studying Greek, had no interest in English grammar:

> Greek has helped me to get beyond my lack of interest in all the different things in English, to the point that and now I can understand it. Different English words, that I don't know, or understand the definition of. It helps me to easily define the meaning, or the words by the structure and what's around it. I am able to read sentences, where I used to have to go back and read it a few times and ask, "What are they saying here?" Instead, I am able to get it much quicker. I'm able to process it quicker, and it's not an active, conscious thing.

Mr. Charles found that Greek aided his understanding of his:

> . . . primary language: being able to argue persuasively through better understanding English. I took Greek later in life and it helped with sentence structures. I am a Teaching Assistant, and it is fun and I enjoy it—but I discovered that, first, the students don't know what a noun is . . . or a subject. And second, idioms are very frustrating. English is highly idiomatic. All language is highly idiomatic. Just imagine being a foreigner to English. [Greek] makes people much more aware of their language.

After doing some follow-up studies on students that had

taken Latin from him, Mr. David observed:

> I found that they were among the top students in Language Arts
> and English Writing Classes. In speaking to English teachers
> who later had some of my students, they indicated that these
> students were very proficient in their writing/compositions as-
> signments. Their knowledge and correct usage of English gram-
> mar was especially noted. I, myself, have learned more about
> English grammar, syntax and word derivation from my studies
> in Latin than in any other courses even though I have a BA de-
> gree with a major in English.

Ms. Edwards, loves teaching Latin:

> . . . because the students seemed to love making all the connec-
> tions with English and ancient culture. They were always saying,
> "Oh, so that is why . . ." My students informed me—often and
> with great pride—that their performance in AP English was
> awesome after having had AP Latin. Their knowledge of scan-
> sion, figurae, and general literary analysis was a great asset in
> their study of English literature. This was the same in their Eng-
> lish essays—one understands the antecedents of pronouns in
> English when the concept has been mastered in Latin.

When asked to describe any changes in her ability to understand other subjects since studying Latin, Ms. Edwards
replied, "I benefited from Latin's structure in my approach to
teaching English, and I used it in presenting parts of speech to
students who should have already known them (but didn't) before I could teach them how to write."

Mr. George found that Latin helped him to "cultivate the
ability to suspend conceptual lines of thought, while one waits
for a verb, for example, and simply to cogitate in a less linear
fashion than English often demands." And Ms. Ida, Ms. Lewis,
and Ms. Mary all specifically mentioned that one obvious ad-

vantage from studying Latin was an increased vocabulary.

In this third section the responses of participants who experienced or observed how Classical languages impacted learning other languages are set forth. The number and variety of the languages acquired by participants that were so impacted is as wide and diverse as I had anticipated would be the case.

How Classical Languages Impact Other Subjects

The following subjects were specifically listed by the participants to have been positively impacted, and made easier to learn because of Latin and/or Greek: math, law, medicine, "various scientific fields," history, politics, archaeology, composition, literature, modern languages (especially Romance languages, in particular: Spanish, French, Italian, Portuguese, Romanian); classical authors; Western culture; physiology; grammar; vocabulary; and music.

Mr. David described how some of his Latin students "have gone into law, medicine and various scientific fields and have become quite successful."

Ms. Edwards believed:

> Knowing Latin literature has helped me with various aspects of lifelong learning. Knowing Roman history has been telling in understanding some of the political issues of the modern world (knowing that nothing really changes, would be implied here). It has also created an interest in archeology, which I studied at Oxford and would have pursued in greater depth, were I younger.

Classical authors were cited by Mr. George, who said, "Reading Latin authors (whether Livy, Vergil, Cicero, Tacitus, or Augustine) has informed my understanding of history, politics, mythology, theology, ethics, and philosophy."

Mr. Henry found that the syntax of both Latin and Greek is almost mathematical, and helped him "to be able to think more clearly, and get better grades in other subjects such as math and science."

Ms. John had Latin and Greek students who not only "scored much higher on SAT tests," but also students in her accelerated beginning Latin class for graduate students who came from fields such as English Comp-Lit, and modern language. These students were required to take her course:

> Since they had not had previous experience in taking Latin and needed to know it for their fields. The students I had in that class over a period of 20 years, felt that they were far better equipped to understand the language background of the work they were dealing with. That was across the board, in all those fields that were required to take Latin. I also think it extends to basic math, because logic is depended upon in translating from Latin to English in a way that doesn't necessarily occur in a modern language. One not only has to unpack the inflected endings of the words because Latin and Greek are highly inflected, but you have to know how those words are used in a sentence so that you can translate it appropriately and correctly. I think I have read just about every Latin and Greek author on the reading list. It opens up a whole world of novelty and interest.

Mr. Lewis discovered that Greek introduced him to vast array of literature he had never experienced—and especially interesting was the study of Western culture:

> It expands my enjoyment of reading, my vocabulary, my understanding of historical context, allusions, even for popular fiction such as *The DaVinci Code*. As I tell my students, Latin connects to virtually everything in the world, somehow, and in class we

often go off on tangents that don't seem like they would have anything to do with Latin, but they do. A classical education just gives one a larger worldview because of everything that developed into the Western tradition that can trace its origins to the Classical and Judeo-Christian traditions.

Ms. Lewis, the homeschooling mother, discovered that "the study of Latin enabled us to understand the English language with a high level of achievement in vocabulary, reading, Classical literature, math and even music."

When participants were asked if Latin and/or Greek aided in learning, math was often mentioned. Mr. Paul felt that classical language mastery was "similar to Euclidean geometry, which lays a foundation, and then builds step-by-step," and that, "to learn Greek or Latin, you have to learn a very structured and ordered language." Others also noted that, because these two languages are so compact, often the verb or an infinitive is left out, and the translator is required to supply it, as in the case of *vellem mortuuos* cited above, where the infinitive (or sometimes an auxiliary verb) has been elided (meaning: left out). Thus, the translator must supply the English words necessary to complete the sentence.

A fourth category that was mentioned significantly by participants is the impact of classical languages on culture, both ancient and modern. Only three participants' voices are heard here.

Classical Languages and Culture

Mr. Frank found these two to be opposite sides of the same coin:

It is hard for me to differentiate between the study of Latin as a language and the authors one reads when learning Latin. Many Latin authors were synthesizers of Greek thought; their prominence in subsequent medieval, Renaissance and Enlightenment thinking have allowed me to enter these later periods with confidence and a common intellectual tradition.

The humanist spirit of the Latin authors was influential in Mr. George's "journey of lifelong learning and in my conception of liberal education and its place in society. There is a texture of thought—quite apart from the substance—which rubs off on those who read and love Latin literature."

His thoughts were echoed and expanded on by Ms. Nancy:

A translation of Cicero isn't as good as the real thing; a translation of Catullus does not hold his pain and passion the same way. No translation in any medium could top the incredible sci-fi action of the sea serpents swallowing up Laocoön and his sons in the *Aeneid*.

A category that emerged similar to but distinct from the impact of classical languages on learning other languages was that of the influence having taken a classical language has on the desire to learn more additional languages. This correlation had a 73% positive response from participants, while, including Greek and Latin, 100% of the participants had taken more than one language, and mentioned that Greek and Latin made learning other languages much easier.

Classical Languages and Modern Languages

A fifth category or theme mentioned by seven of the sixteen participants was that of the impact of classical languages on the desire to learn modern languages that is seemingly provoked. To preface this phenomenon, Mr. King stated, "In studying the history of English, Latin has had a huge influence. If classical languages help with English, that only means that the study of one language helps in the study of another."

Eleven out of the sixteen participants (Dr. Adams, Mr. Charles, Mr. David, Ms. Edwards, Ms. Frank, Mr. George, Ms. Ida, Ms. John, Mr. King, and Ms. Lewis) found that having studied a classical language helped them learn modern languages with much more ease. Between them they had studied in order of number of times mentioned: French (6), German (6), Spanish (6), Italian (4), Portuguese (2), Russian (2), Hebrew (1), Old Norse (1), and Swedish (1).

Specifically, Dr. Adams found that the grammar built into Latin helped with learning German and French. He also said, "I think ultimately just learning another language distances you from your own language, and thus really helps in understanding your native language."

But more particularly to the point, Ms. Edwards, who had studied eight languages, commented on the impact of Latin on both her and her students' experience with Latin and other languages:

> Knowledge of the structure of [Latin] has created in me more of an interest in all languages. And, in addition, my students who have studied other foreign languages reported that they understood German grammar, for instance, so much better, after understanding how grammar works in Latin. The knowledge of cognates is of course the primary contribution here.

Mr. Charles, who along with two other participants has studied eight languages, stated that, "Latin is helpful in learning languages: it helps being able to operate within a foreign language: constructs, and how you form them. It forces you to learn study habits."

He concluded with a thought that resonates with my experience: "It is not difficult learning more than one language at a time. You just have to learn to compartmentalize." I studied Greek and Hebrew in graduate school in the same semester. On Tuesday, I wrote from right to left, and on Thursday I wrote from left to right, in two different alphabets, with totally different vowel paradigms and grammar structures—and compartmentalizing *was* the key.

For the majority of the participants, studying Latin has opened doors to the study of linguistics and other languages. For example, Ms. John, who started Latin in high school and had four years of Latin, also studied French and German, and believed "it was a lot easier learning those languages, because I already knew Latin."

These findings were especially interesting to me, having studied eight languages, Latin being the first, then Spanish, French, and Italian, followed by German, Hebrew, Russian and Japanese. It appears that there might be some underlying predilection in some people to learn languages other than their native tongue; and, upon studying one language, an interest is kindled for learning others.

Mr. Paul's interest in Latin began around age ten, when a passage in Latin in a Sherlock Holmes story was encountered that had been left untranslated by the author:

> I soon purchased a Latin dictionary, looked up the mysterious
> sounding words, solved the puzzle of the translation, and was

hooked. When I saw Latin offered as an elective in middle school, my journey into languages began.

RESEARCH QUESTION 2

The second research question addresses how and to what extent a return to a classical curriculum would furnish students with the tools necessary for knowing how to learn, contributes to their ability to think critically, and provides a methodology for mastering all subjects. Interviews were conducted and journals were collected, in which the participants addressed the following:

1. Describe any changes that your classical education had on your ability to understand other subjects.
2. Tell about the ways that your classical education has impacted your education, ability to reason logically, and how it has impacted your lifelong learning.
3. Discuss the impact on education in America should a return to a classical curriculum occur.
4. List some reasons why the classical curriculum has fallen into disfavor in most public schools.

I was not surprised to learn that only one or two of the participants had had anything close to a classical education. And only one offered an opinion as to why the public school system today does not follow a classical curriculum. Ms. John was in a classical program designed to equip her "to go to any college or university in the United States." This program required her to study Latin and English for four years; and to take three years of French, math, and history, among others. When she entered college, she "added Greek to that general background and found that to be an extension of everything I had studied before." She believes that one reason educators do not offer a classical curriculum is that they "did not have it themselves, in many cases, and as time goes on fewer and fewer people in education have any kind of background (in classical education) at all."

Yet her experience has been that there is great value in a classical education:

> The truth is you learn self-discipline when you learn Greek and Latin, and self-discipline helps you learn anything. I wish Latin was more prevalent in high schools today than it is. I believe it is absolutely beneficial to students who are going on to college, and also for students who are going out into the real world. But, unfortunately, Latin is a low priority in the majority of schools.

Mr. Charles is impressed

> . . . by the student who leads the fundraiser for Latin Club, the student who decided to participate in a contest, the student who brings me an awesome project, the students who actually prepare for the quizzes and tests. For most of my students, Latin is, indeed, a handmaiden to their interests, and I as a teacher aim to help them use it well. I also have had classes where maybe a fourth of the class does its homework and prepares for quizzes/tests. These kids have the theory that if no one does it, it doesn't matter . . . I am always frustrated by the fact that none of my students make Latin a priority in their daily studying and homework routines. I took a survey, and Latin was fourth from the top.

Ms. Edward's enthusiasm was evident as she described how her students seem to take pride in their success at a subject that is challenging and that gives them confidence to meet more academic challenges later on. She concluded by noting that many students have told her that "the process of learning first year Latin vocabulary and grammar has been invaluable to them when they take anatomy and physiology and chemistry."

As stated above, the categories that emerged in this study were divided into positive and negative responses. Below are the negative responses in reference to both research questions. Though these participants had comments that were counter to the others, nonetheless, they provide a balance and much insight into the research questions posed by this study.

Negative Input Regarding Research Questions 1 and 2

Although the majority of the participants—twelve out of sixteen—had nothing but positive input in reference to the benefits of classical language acquisition, the remaining four had some reservations. These four agreed that Latin and Greek were worth studying, but they offered the following comments:

Dr. Adams: "I haven't had anyone come forward and make those kinds of statements," [that is, that Latin or Greek had impacted their ability to learn other subjects].

Ms. Edwards: "I do not really think that the structure of the language, per se, has had as much of an impact as knowing the thoughts and writing styles of the great Latin writers, poets and playwrights."

Conversely, Mr. Otto cautioned that there is an element of learning that

> we, as teachers, cannot reach. It is the element of how a student may want to connect the parts of what he/she has learned, and understand the big picture, rather than memorizing for the task

at hand.

After teachers give their students as much practice as possible putting accusatives and ablatives with prepositions, but until there is a desire or even a recognition [sic] on their part that this is part of a bigger picture, the elements often remain as disjointed pieces of information. As a result, he lamented, "Some students will always give me sentences with every noun in the nominative case, and every verb in the infinitive or first person singular."

There is no substitute for understanding what the lessons are designed to teach: how to use the endings and forms in translation. Memorizing paradigms does not ensure that those forms communicate anything. The student who has memorized endings will be able to edit something—but a student cannot edit before understanding how to produce. So, time spent helping students produce Latin (speaking, reading, and writing) is a necessary precursor to editing for which knowing endings will help.

Ms. John thought that although Latin had an impact on learning other languages, she did not believe it extended to science. She also failed to see how studying Latin:

> . . . would aid in understanding other subjects or studying them. Latin is a language like any other. Even its status as a dead language is in no way unique as dozens of languages join it in that status every decade, unfortunately. Latin is no more or less "logical" than any other language. What may happen is that students taught in a grammar-driven Latin class may learn some analytical skills as they laboriously translate from Latin to English, a pointless exercise that never helped my Latin. Certainly the concepts of case, voice, mood, tense, and so forth are interesting, at least for those who acquire some knowledge of them—most former Latin "scholars," as they're called, learned nothing like

that, being able only to shout "amo, amas, amat" with great pride. If these concepts help with English, that only means that the study of one language helps in the study of another and, sadly, much English grammar has been forced into a Latin mold.

With reference to research question number two regarding a classical curriculum, Mr. Paul was very adamant that it would never happen, although it was not clear to me if he was describing things as they are, or things he was in favor of:

> A traditional classical curriculum isn't possible in postmodern circumstances. There is too much other material to cover, too many new disciplines compete for attention, and curriculum based on precise language training, including Latin and/or Greek would lead to better communication across the board— better attention to the meaning of words and phrases, political discourse about something other than buzzwords. Nationalism and Modernism militated against transnational and fossilized classics. New disciplines required curricular time, and the classics were masculine and elitist—ergo feminists and egalitarians opposed the classics viscerally.

Ms. Nancy stated that she was only interested in how "students perform in my class, what techniques work best for each kid, how I can get them more engaged in the language, etc."

Her final comments were directed at the "bean counters and the puppet masters behind No Child Left Behind" that she was "so darned tired of"—and said she refuses "to make my course something for statistics." Ms. Nancy's Web site that she maintains touts Latin as a source of all the positive benefits cited by the majority of the participants. Her Web site lists the following reasons to study Latin: (a) "Latin develops a person's English"; (b) "Greek and Latin provide a solid foundation for the acquisition of other languages"; (c) "reading, writing, and translating Greek and Latin sharpen the mind"; (d) "the civilizations of Greece and Rome link us with cultures of 57 nations on four continents"; (e) "acquaintance with ancient cultures promotes tolerance and understanding"; (f) "test scores in elementary schools have demonstrated the value of early language training"; and, (g) "students of diverse nationalities benefit from the study of Latin." (Barrett, 2007, cited on Ms. Nancy's Web site).

Artifacts

A wide variety of artifacts are employed by classical language teachers to aid in remembering, translating and assimilating the words, endings, and grammar involved. Examples are to be found in APPENDIX E. They demonstrate what documents might typically be found in the classroom, such as study sheets, syllabuses, and vocabulary lists.

SUMMARY

In this chapter, the findings of the research study were presented. Broad categories included (a) the impact on understanding and using English; (b) learning other languages; (c) the benefits to studying Latin and/or Greek that were observed by participants in both their own education and that of their students; (d) ease in acquiring other subjects such as math, science, history, and culture; (e) reasons why so many educators today have not adopted a classical education curriculum; and, (f) the differences in the impact of Latin versus Greek in ease of acquiring other subjects.

The interviews provided a context in which to visualize the teaching of Latin, Greek and classical education, and provided support for the statements recorded in the interviews. Together, the data sources explained, described, and validated the phenomenon of the impact of classical languages on learning other subjects.

Interviews and journals revealed much information regarding the impact of classical languages on learning. The importance they attributed to classical languages and classical education was dependent on the value they perceived in the classroom and in their lives; the internal and external pressures from students; society; the No Child Left Behind Act; and other institutional mandates, subtle and overt; and factors they believed competed for their attention.

In the next chapter, the data analyzed in this chapter will be applied to the research problem to see if the participants' testimony supports the statement of Dorothy L. Sayers, that Latin is useful in reducing the pain of learning any other subject by 50%.

V

SUMMARY, CONCLUSIONS, AND RECOMMENDATIONS

INTRODUCTION

This study questioned if and to what extent the study of classical Latin and/or Greek would simplify the study of any other academic subject, and sought to explore how and to what extent a return to a classical curriculum would furnish students with the tools necessary for knowing how to learn, contribute to their ability to think critically, and provide a methodology for mastering all subjects.

To determine the effect of a classical education on the participants in this study, interviews were conducted and journals were collected, in which the participants, consisting of sixteen Latin and/or Greek teachers and students, addressed the following:

1. Did you notice any change in your students' quiz/test scores in other subjects after they took Latin?
2. Describe any changes in your ability to understand other subjects since studying Latin.

3. Tell about the ways that knowing Latin has impacted your education, ability to reason logically, and how it has impacted your lifelong learning.

The discussion that follows sets forth the findings of this study, offers conclusions, raises questions, and presents implications that emerged from the study. Also, the pages below present a summary and the conclusions that were reached from data gathered and analyzed during the course of this study. The conclusions that I reached will be discussed, along with the implications for general practice, and some recommendations for future research.

Answering the Research Questions

Even though the purpose and original intent of this study was to explore the impact of Latin, Greek, and a Classical Education on learning other subjects, the ensuing data gathering, categorizing, sorting, sifting, and analysis of date resulted in several unexpected shifts in the focus of the study. Although the core of this study remains centered on the original research problem, a number of important themes emerged.

These unanticipated themes arose repeatedly in the interviews and journals and were integrated into the study: (a) The impact of studying Latin and/or Greek on understanding and using English; (b) the specific subjects impacted by studying Latin and/or Greek, such as math, law, medicine, "various scientific fields," history, politics, archaeology, composition, literature, modern languages (especially Romance languages, in particular: Spanish, French, Italian, Portuguese, Romanian), classical authors, Western culture, physiology, grammar, vocabulary, and music; (c) reasons that a classical education curriculum is rarely taught; (d) differences in the impact on Latin versus that of Greek in the ease of acquiring other subjects; and (e) problems that exist but would not change if public schools decided to switch to a classical curriculum or even just to offer Latin and/or Greek.

Other issues that were discussed in CHAPTER 1 above and that were thought to possibly affect the literature on research in classical languages were not considered factors by the participants. Neither were they even mentioned by any participants in their journals: (a) budgets for a Latin program may or may not be equal to that spent on other languages; (b) there are many fewer games, records, published activities, or popular books translated into Latin than there are for other languages; (c) conditions, climate, lighting, environment, and distractions in the classroom; (d) teacher training and quality of teaching styles as well as individual attention and instruction; (e) provision for learning styles; (f) equality in testing; (g) variation and equality in the manner in which the material is taught; and (h) the manner in which data is recorded, collated, and transferred from numbers to narrative, and disseminated.

DISCUSSION

This section discusses the findings of the study, offers conclusions, raises questions, and presents implications that emerged from the study, beginning with five themes that became apparent from analysis of the data and that were presented in detail in CHAPTER 4. The themes revolve around the teachers' perceptions relating to: classical education; conceptualizations of classical language instruction; impacts on understanding English grammar, and vocabulary; impacts on learning other languages; and the similarities between Latin and Greek as to their impact on learning other subjects. The original focus of this study was explored fully, but the focus shifted onto related topics as data was gathered and analyzed as will be seen, since these topics are discussed below in the order they were presented above.

Few current studies could be found related to the themes of this study. However, the voices of the participants herein contribute the wealth of their collective experience to the theoretical literature, and their thoughts will be compared to gain a clearer understanding of the impact of classical languages on learning other subjects.

Classical Languages and Goals

The literature, as well as the findings of this study, indicates there are ambiguities and tensions in the field related to the impact of classical languages on acquiring other subjects. Participants in this study confirmed varied, even conflicting, goals for studying Latin and/or Greek. Given the initial focus of this study, a discussion of the literature was included in CHAPTER 2, citing documents from 1935 to 2007, to demonstrate the validity of classical languages as facilitators of learning.

In contrast to the literature, participants in this study did not often refer to the benefits of classical languages as an aid to improving SAT scores—or as a source for derivatives that aid in English vocabulary. In fact, some participants did not seem to be familiar with the evidence set forth in the literature on those two topics, while others seemed to hold up these known benefits up as significant, but not as the primary goal of learning classical languages.

Still others were less interested in the side benefits to learning Latin and/or Greek, such as increased mental capacity, and more interested in promoting as the primary goal, entrée to the culture and literature of ancient civilizations. Four of the participants perceived Latin and/or Greek as ends in themselves, rather than just studies that opened doors to critical thinking, understanding English, vocabulary improvement, higher SAT scores, and other benefits.

Participant responses are divided into three broad categories: how classical languages have had a positive effect on their personal lifelong learning; the impact on their students' achievement; and the manner in which their understanding of English has been improved. These findings reflect the contemporary literature. These three themes will be explored in the discussion that follows.

Study findings disclosed other tertiary goals: reasons that a classical education curriculum is rarely taught; differences in the impact of Latin versus Greek in ease of acquiring other subjects; and problems that exist but would not change if public schools decided to switch to a classical curriculum or even just to offer Latin and/or Greek. The discussion that follows will also address those goals that twelve out of the sixteen participants agree have impacted their lives and the lives of their students in a positive manner. Even though the remaining four were reluctant to agree without certain qualifications, their comments were not negations of that premise. More of the participants in this study agree than disagree that both Latin and Greek are equally beneficial.

IMPLICATIONS FOR GENERAL PRACTICE

The previous four chapters of this study have been focused on exploring the impact of classical Latin, Greek, and the classical education model on the ability of students to acquire other subjects through examining the current low performance rates at United States public schools, by comparing and contrasting current practice with the history of Latin and Greek in education and through reviewing the extant literature on these subjects. Kennedy (2006) documented in his quantitative dissertation how for centuries Latin teachers have observed improved English reading and writing skills, as well as the development of logic and reasoning faculties. Having taught both classical Latin and Greek, I have collected data from other classical language teachers, shedding more light on these phenomena.

This study has set forth the collected experience of sixteen teachers and students who have spoken and written on how classical languages have impacted their education, and how they have eased their ability to learn a myriad of subjects. A classically educated citizenry would be composed of thoughtful people who know how to learn, who have the tools to maintain their ability to think freely, and would provide a methodology for mastering all subjects.

The interviews and journals were ultimately divided into quite different categories than those anticipated by the original questions. Recurring themes occurred as represented by the following six categories: (a) the benefits to studying Latin and/or Greek that have been observed by participants, in their students and, in their own education; (b) the impact of studying Latin and/or Greek on understanding and using English; (c) the impact of studying Latin and/or Greek on acquiring other subjects, such as math, science, history, culture, and other languages; (d) reasons that a classical education curriculum is rarely taught; (e) differences in the impact of Latin versus Greek in ease of acquiring other subjects, and, (f) problems that exist but would not change if public schools decided to switch to a classical curriculum or even just to offer Latin and/or Greek.

The research statement that formed the basis for this study was "It is not known if and to what extent the study of Classical Latin and/or Greek will simplify the study of any other academic subject." This study had the following two research questions:

1. How and to what extent does a basic knowledge of classical Latin and/or Greek simplify the study of almost any other subject?
2. How and to what extent would a return to a classical curriculum furnish students with the tools necessary for knowing how to learn, contribute to their ability to think critically, and provide a methodology for mastering all subjects?

The focus of the data gathered was to provide a basis for analyzing the perspectives of various individuals who had taken a classical language, to provide information that I could reflect upon and write about in a journal, and to fully address the research questions. What follows will be divided into two sections, each section dealing with each of the two research questions, ending with a summary of the findings of the research study.

Research Question 1

The first research question addressed the impact of a basic knowledge of classical Latin and/or Greek on simplifying the study of almost any other subject, and was primarily answered by Latin/Greek teachers, former teachers, former students, and me.

Interviews were conducted and journals were collected, in which the participants addressed the following: (a) Did you notice any change in your students' quiz/test scores in other subjects after they took Latin? (b) Describe any changes in your ability to understand other subjects since studying Latin. (c) Tell about the ways that knowing Latin has impacted your education, ability to reason logically, and how it has impacted your lifelong learning.

Impacts of Classical Languages on Learning

Although one of the purposes for carrying out this study was to gain an understanding of how adult educators perceive the impact of classical languages, during the interviews, participants spoke about overarching goals for the field of adult education. From their responses, three broad categories were identified: how classical languages have had a positive effect on their personal lifelong learning; the impact on their students' achievement; and the manner in which their understanding of English has been improved. These three categories are described in the following section. The first theme to emerge from the study was a positive effect upon learning in general from having studied a classical language.

Positive Effects of Classical Languages

Twelve out of the sixteen participants agreed that classical languages have impacted their lives and the lives of their students in a positive manner. The remaining four were reluctant to agree without qualifications, but neither were their comments negations of that premise.

To summarize, benefits of learning classical languages are: exercising the mind; being able to process reading; comprehension of other subjects; reading the original for nuances; overarching subjects and integrative ideas; gaining a catalyst for understanding other subjects; expanding your mind and thinking abilities; aids learning; helping students with what they communicate in a globalized world; engaging with non-Western culture; laying the foundation for other fields; success produces confidence; linguistic skills; memorization; mental exercise; gaining honors in college; understanding of language; better test scores; ability to reason logically; obtaining scholarships; bringing order to disorganized thinking; giving students critical thinking skills; and providing a background in common Latin and Greek phrases often used in English.

Classical Languages as an Aid to Proficiency in English

Common themes provided by participants include (a) improvement in reading, writing style, grammar, and comprehension; (b) being able to read more carefully; (c) ability to memorize and figure out how to learn new subject matter; (d) skill in understanding construction and sentences; (e) thinking beyond the idioms and cultural expressions of English; (f) ability to understand one's primary language; (g) being able to argue persuasively through better understanding of English; (h) help in understanding idiomatic phrases; (i) honors in language arts and English writing classes; (j) proficiency in writing/compositions and essay assignments; (k) knowledge and correct usage of English grammar; (l) improvement in English grammar, syntax and word derivation; (m) gaining an understanding of the connections between English and ancient culture; (n) a knowledge of scansion, figurae, and general literary analysis useful in studying English literature; (o) grasping the concepts of such terms as antecedents of pronouns in English and parts of speech; and (p) an increased vocabulary through derivatives.

The following table is included to set forth in a single location the various data collected from participants, and to illustrate the similarities in their experiences:

PARTICIPANT	EFFECTS	OL=OTHER LANGUAGES	SPECIFIC SUBJECTS
Dr. Adams	English; read more carefully; logic; memorization	Greek and Latin. OL: German, French	Have seen no impact on other subjects.
Mr. Baker	English; processing, comprehension, vocabulary; logic	Greek and Latin	Greek as overarching effect tying all other subjects together
Mr. David	English: writing, correct grammar	OL: Spanish and French	Law; medicine; science; philosophy

Table 2. Effects of Classical Languages as Viewed by Participants

PARTICIPANT	EFFECTS	OL=OTHER LANGUAGES	SPECIFIC SUBJECTS
Ms. Edwards	English: composition; confidence	OL: French, German, Italian, Swedish, Russian, Spanish, Old Norse	Learning; Roman history; politics; archaeology; Latin literature; mythology; theology; ethics; philosophy
Mr. Frank	English: prose; Latin authors	8 OL	Classical authors
Mr. George	English: cognates; logic	OL: Spanish, French, Italian, Portuguese	Latin authors; humanism
Mr. Henry	English; logic	Greek and Latin	Arts and sciences; math; SAT; honor students
Ms. Ida	English	OL	Ancient authors
Ms. John	English: SAT; logic; discipline	OL: French, German	Math
Mr. King	English; composition; literature	OL	Anatomy; physiology; Roman history
Ms. Lewis	English: vocabulary	OL	Worldview; honors
Ms. Mary	English; GPA; scholarships	OL: Greek	Academics; literature; math; music
Ms. Nancy	English; Latin literature	OL	Little impact on anything else; SAT
Mr. Otis	English; critical thinking; discipline; memorization	OL	Math; science; history
Mr. Paul	English: vocab. composition; logic; critical thinking; memorization; lifelong learning	OL: German, French, Italian, Hebrew, Greek, Latin, Spanish, Japanese	All other subjects

As seen in the table above, the impact of classical languages on other subjects included: English (16); logic (7); math (4); Latin literature (3); lifelong learning (2); Roman history (2); classical authors (2); history (2); mythology (2); theology (2); law (1), medicine (1), and "various scientific fields" (1); modern political issues (1); archaeology (1); ethics (1); philosophy (1); humanism (1); anatomy (1); physiology (1); chemistry (1); Latin and Greek authors (1); literature (1); Western culture (1); and a larger worldview (multiculturalism) (1).

One participant stated he hoped that in the future, teachers would help students understand all subjects more clearly by making connections between classes, rather than each being compartmentalized and separate. Another participant saw connections between "the study of Latin" and such disparate subjects as "English . . . classical literature, math and even music."

All sixteen participants agreed that classical languages had an impact on the desire to learn modern languages. Eleven of the participants found that having studied a classical language helped them learn modern languages with much more ease. Between them they had studied French, German, Hebrew, Italian, Japanese, Old Norse, Portuguese, Russian, Spanish, and Swedish.

Research Question 2

The second research question addresses how and to what extent a return to a classical curriculum would furnish students with the tools necessary for knowing how to learn, contribute to their ability to think critically, and provide a methodology for mastering all subjects. From the interviews and journals, data emerged regarding the participants' perception of how a classical education had changed their ability to understand other subjects, their education, ability to reason logically, and lifelong learning; what the impact on education in America might be, should a return to a classical curriculum occur; and reasons why the classical curriculum has fallen into disfavor.

Only one or two of the participants had had anything close to a classical education, and only one offered an opinion as to why the public school system today does not follow a classical curriculum. Ms. John believes that one reason educators do not offer a classical curriculum is that they "did not have it themselves, in many cases, and as time goes on fewer and fewer people in education have any kind of background (in classical education) at all." Yet her experience has been that there is great value in a classical education. But, unfortunately, Latin is a low priority in the majority of schools.

If current policy changed, and a switch was made to a classical curriculum, or even if Latin and/or Greek were offered in public schools, there would still be a number of barriers to seeing improvement in other subjects, according to several participants. There is a lot of pressure on the students who are trying to get accepted into a major university, causing them, as Mr. Baker noted, to become

> calculating, and given the advice they get from counselors, other teachers, and parents . . . it's no wonder they see Latin as "just an elective that better not screw up my grade point average while I focus on pre-calculus and AP chemistry."

Students state very clearly that languages are not one of the core subjects and thus not worth taking. Latin is often viewed as elitist and unnecessary, since, as they say, "Everyone speaks English these days. Why would you study a dead language?" Students cannot help but notice that the SAT and ACT tests only English and math, sending a not so subtle message that helps to underscore this attitude. Knowing they will not be tested on foreign language mastery, languages are relegated to the elective category.

Latin is not a priority, nor is any elective anymore, after the No Child Left Behind Act In the United States, many districts don't even require a second language to graduate. Participants see that society does not value the learning of a second language, and that cue is picked-up on by students. As schools face the threat of losing funding and try to avoid being shut down for not making annual yearly progress, students now spend the bulk of their homework time, upwards of seven hours a day on math and science. Whatever time is left over is spent on English studies, with little time for Latin or anything else. Many participants speculate on what kind of free spirits and broad minds we will produce for this next generation. And several have switched from teaching Latin to other subjects, "given the current climate" and are bailing out of the classics programs.

Participants relate how their Latin students all worry about their math and science homework. Even their best students do not make Latin a priority because they have high level science and math courses. No matter how long the Latin teacher makes a homework assignment, or how difficult a particular grammar point is, the students wait until homeroom to try to complete their homework—or worse, copy it—or study for a quiz. Students do a terrible job of translating it in homeroom and work to "get it done" instead of getting it correct.

Participants lamented, "The math and science teachers are all business, and the kids are petrified of blinking the wrong way in those classes—doing 45 minutes of boring repetitive math problems, but not a fraction of that on a Latin translation." One participant described using strict grading to force students to actually study before a quiz, to help them take Latin seriously, rather than lowering the bar, and passing everyone. Counselors are telling them that everything is more important than Latin for their future. He argues that students will produce what you expect. The higher the demands, the better quality of work you will receive. Lower the bar, and they may act like they do, but they do not respect you. Their grades must truly reflect their knowledge and their effort.

The majority of participants agreed, but Mr. Charles voiced the opposite opinion:

> Doing work out of fear is not learning. It is externally focused behavior based on fear, and should not be encouraged. Surely our world is full enough of fear motivation without teachers, of all people, joining that sad chorus.

Mr. Charles appeared eager to share his views on student motivation as he noted that most of his students are really busy with sports, clubs, jobs, family, and relationships, among others. What these students do for Latin class is impressive in the light of none of them having expressed an interest in majoring in Latin—the student who does all the work even if language isn't his/her forte.

Ms. King did not hesitate to explain her conviction that it is possible to run classes where fun, humor, creativity, kindness, as well as high academic expectations are all present: "I don't think that fun and a rigorous program are mutually exclusive. I doubt my students fear me, but they know that I am serious about my job and about their achievement."

The categories that emerged in this study were divided into positive and negative responses. Below are the negative responses in reference to both research questions. Though these participants had comments that ran counter to the others, they nonetheless provide balance and much insight into the research questions posed by this study.

Negative Input Regarding Research Questions 1 and 2

Although the majority of the participants, twelve out of sixteen, had nothing but positive input in reference to the benefits of classical language acquisition, the remaining four had some reservations. These four agreed that Latin and Greek were worth studying, but they had other comments, ranging from a belief that neither Latin nor Greek had impacted their students' ability to learn other subjects, to the conviction that classical languages do not help teachers understand how to aid students to connect lessons and understand the big picture—students do not understand sentence construction by learning endings. One commented that Latin does not help with subjects such as science, and that Latin is no more or less logical than any other language: if learning the elements of Latin helps with English, that only means that the study of one language helps in the study of another. Another tied a rejection of traditional classical curriculum to postmodern circumstances: because nationalism and modernism have been rejected, dead languages are permanently out of favor, and, since classical subjects are considered masculine and elitist, they are opposed by feminists and egalitarians. One stated that she had no interest at all in how their students perform in other classes, and her only interest was in students' reading what the ancients wrote in their own words, giving students a passion for the language, not an ability to chant nonsensical charts. This same teacher who believes Latin is not a special or exceptionally logical language, has posted SAT statistics and a half-dozen standard reasons for studying Latin on her Web site.

In summary, participants' beliefs about the impact of classical languages being overstated are in the minority. Their perceptions are subjective and based on observations and bad experiences. I agree, however, in part with many of their comments. Having suffered through first year Latin under a mean-spirited, bitter, joyless teacher, Mr. W, it may well be true that Latin itself, as taught by any teacher, is not a panacea, but a language with much promise that needs to be taught well. There are good teachers and bad teachers, inspiring teachers and boring teachers.

One such teacher described by a participant—Mr. Paul—was Mr. X, one of the other Latin teachers at the high school where Mr. Paul taught. Mr. X used to stand at the whiteboard with his back to his class, writing the answers to exercises, without stopping for questions—assuming that what he was doing was actually teaching. Later his students approached Mr. Paul, asking him to explain that week's lessons, saying: "Mr. X just goes on and on, and never pauses to see if we have any questions—he may understand the lesson, but most of the time we have no idea what he is talking about." Mr. X had odd mannerisms that made him the butt of student jokes, and he used such bizarre phrases as, "Your Latin paper looks like my grandmother in a bikini," which caused his students to hate his class. Some of them hated Latin—because of Mr. X.

When Mr. X's confused students came to Mr. Paul after school, Mr. Paul stated that he always took the time to answer their questions and tutored them in whatever topics they hadn't understood because of Mr. X's bad teaching style. After Mr. X was fired, several of his students came into Mr. Paul's class—and began to enjoy Latin for the first time. Mr. X may have known Latin well—but because he was not able to communicate what he knew, he left terrible wreckage in his wake. Learning was not taking place in his classroom; rather, he was talking at his students, writing out meaningless exercises on the board, and throwing information at them.

Bad teaching practice can cause a disconnect when the emphasis is on learning case endings and passing quizzes instead of learning what those endings mean. A mnemonic taught to a student may assist in learning the noun and verb endings, but does very little to aid understanding. The problem for Latin teachers is how to bridge the gap between learning the mnemonic and learning to think in a classical language.

The teacher connection may have a direct bearing on why Dorothy L. Sayers believed Latin would aid in learning other subjects. Having had her mother as her teacher, there may have been a nurturing, bonding effect that caused Dorothy to thrive and to learn quickly. The opposite effect might be achieved if the teacher teaches strictly by rote and drills and does not employ a variety of approaches, and that teacher may negate any potentially positive benefits from Latin.

One participant, Mr. Baker, concluded that teachers should continue to provide a classroom experience that would cause

> students to love your class. They will not remember the periodic table in 20 years, but they will probably encourage their own children to enroll in Latin as they remember how much they loved the class. It is reality.

FUTURE RESEARCH NEEDED

The results of this study indicate that classical languages have a positive impact on learning. This information should be shared with those who are in a position to determine the curriculum at public schools, and who could support and expand existing Latin programs—namely, the parents and administrators. As described in CHAPTER 4 of this study, there are some classical language teachers who disagree, and further research is required into this phenomenon to determine the underlying reasons why classical language students perform so well, and if these results are reproducible or generalizable.

Among the issues discussed in CHAPTER 1 above that were thought to possibly affect the impact of classical languages are: (a) budgets for a Latin program might or might not be equal to that spent on other languages; (b) there are many fewer games, records, published activities, or popular books translated into Latin than there are for other languages; (c) conditions, climate, lighting, environment, and distractions in the classroom; (d) teacher training and quality of teaching styles as well as individual attention and instruction; (e) provision for learning styles; (f) equality in testing; (g) variation and equality in the manner in which the material is taught; and (h) the manner in which data is recorded, collated, and transferred from numbers to narrative, and disseminated. These issues were not considered important factors by the participants and lightly touched on, if at all, in this study. Further studies could be done to determine if indeed these issues are factors in improving learning.

CONCLUSIONS

In this chapter, the findings of the research study based on analysis of interview transcripts, journals, and field notes were presented. Findings were discussed by categories derived from sifting all comments and allowing the voices of participants to be heard. Data in the first section focused on the impact of classical languages on learning other subjects. Analysis of the data revealed that participants were generally very persuaded that the impact was of a positive nature. Broad categories included the impact on English, learning other languages, the benefits to studying Latin and/or Greek that have been observed by participants in their students and in their own education; the impact of studying Latin and/or Greek on understanding and using English and the impact of studying Latin and/or Greek on acquiring other subjects such as math, science, history, culture, and other languages; the reasons why so many educators today have not adopted a classical education curriculum; and the differences in the impact of Latin versus Greek in ease of acquiring other subjects.

Participants also had negative input, which was commented upon. The final section dealt briefly with artifacts gathered from participants. These themes that emerged as data was analyzed revealed the high standards of excellence required by Latin and Greek teachers for their students. School leaders and teachers who participated in this study were in a continuous process of striving for improvement through professional development, and collaboration in the midst of a culture of expectations and discipline. The interviews provided a context in which to visualize the teaching of Latin, Greek and classical education, and provided support for the statements recorded in the interviews. Together, the data sources explained, described, and validated the phenomenon of the impact of classical languages on learning other subjects. Although the number of participants is not large, one measure of the value of the collected data is the knowledge, expertise, and wisdom possessed by fourteen teachers who collectively have over two hundred years of classroom experience informing their comments.

Interviews with and journals by participants revealed much information regarding the impact of classical languages on learning, and their perceptions of the importance of classical languages and classical education. The importance they attributed to classical languages was dependent on the value they perceived in the classroom and in their lives; the internal and external pressures from students; society; the No Child Left Behind Act; and other institutional mandates, subtle and overt; and factors they believed competed for their attention.

A return to classical languages and classical curricula has proven beneficial in many schools in America in producing higher SAT scores and improved learning. Further research could be done into the effects that a return to the lost tools of learning—and Latin in particular—would have upon the crisis in the public school systems. A study could be done to determine the reasons why classical language students score so much higher on SAT tests. Further research could determine if a return to core subjects and the proven classical curriculum could allow students who are not learning how to learn, and who are not able to compete at the college level, to succeed. Future studies could reveal whether a return to Latin would, in effect, be a return to higher academic achievement.

APPENDIX A

DERIVATIVES

PREFIXES	DERIVATIVE	MEANING	EXAMPLE
a-, ab-	Latin	off, from, down, away	abduct, avert
a-, an-	Greek	not, without, less	abiotic, anaerobic
ad-	Latin	to, attached to	adsorption
aer-	Greek	air	aerobic
amphi-	Greek	both, about, around	amphibian
ana-	Latin	away, through, again	analysis
andro-	Greek	man, male	androgens
angio-	Greek	a closed container	angiospermae
anthropo-	Greek	referring to man	anthropology
ant-, anti-	Greek	against, away, opposite	antibiosis
ante-	Latin	before	anteroom
ap-, apo-	Latin	from, off, separate	apogee
aqua-	Latin	water	aquatic
archeo-	Greek	ancient, primitive	archeology
arthri-	Greek	joint, jointed	arthritis
aureo-	Latin	gold-colored	aureomycin
auto-	L./Gk.	self	autoimmune
bi-	Latin	two, twice, double	bipolar, binocular
bio-, bios-	Greek	related to life	biology, biocidal
blasto-	L./Gk.	embryonic layer or cell	blastomere
brachy-	Greek	short	brachycephalic
brady-	Greek	slow, slowness	bradycardia
bry-, bryo-	Greek	moss, mossy	bryophyte
calix-	Latin	cuplike	calyx
canis-	Latin	dog	canine
cardia-	L./Gk.	heart	cardiac
carn-	Latin	flesh	carnivore
carp-	Latin	wrist, bones	carpal
cata-	Greek	decomposition	catabolism
cell-	Latin	small room	cellular, cellar, cell
cephal-	Latin	head	cephalic
chloro-	Greek	green	chlorophyll
chroma-	Greek	color	chromatic
chron-	Greek	time	chronometer
circum-	Latin	around, near, about	circumnavigate

PREFIXES	DERIVATIVE	MEANING	EXAMPLE
col-, com-	Latin	with, together	combine, collide
contra-	Latin	against	contradict
crypto-	Greek	hidden	cryptic
cyano-	Greek	dark blue	cyanobacteria
cyst-	Greek	bladder	cystitis
cyt-, cyte-, cyto-	Greek	cell, hollow vessel	cytology
de-	Latin	undoing, removal	dehydration
den-, dent-	Latin	tooth	dentition
dendro-	Greek	tree	dendrite
derm-, derma-	Greek	skin, hide	dermatitis
deut-, deutero-	Greek	second, secondary	deuterium
di-	Greek	double, twice, two	disaccharide
dia-	Greek	through, across	diameter
diplo-	Greek	twofold, double	diploid
dis-	Latin	apart, away	dissolve
dorm-	Latin	to sleep	dormant, dormitory
drom-	Greek	a running, racing	dromedary
e-, ec-	Latin	out, out of	effluent
eco-	Greek	house, environment	ecology
ecto-	Greek	outside	ectoderm
en-, endo-	Greek	within, internal	endoskeleton
entero-	Greek	intestine	enterocolitis
entomo-	Latin	insect	entomology
eo-, eos-	Greek	the dawn	Eocene, eohippus
epi-	Greek	upon, above, top	epidermis
erythro-	Greek	red	erythrocyte
eu-	Greek	proper, true, good	euphemism
ex-	Latin	out, from	excise
exo-	Greek	outer, external	exoskeleton
extra-	Latin	outside of, beyond	extracellular
flagell-	Latin	whip, whiplike	flagellum
gamo-	Greek	sexual union	gamogenesis
gastero-, gastro-	Greek	stomach, belly	gastroenteritis
geno-	Latin	origin, development	genotype
ge-, geo-	Greek	earth	geology
glu-, glyco-	Greek	sweet, sugar	glucose, glycogen

PREFIXES	DERIVATIVE	MEANING	EXAMPLE
gon-, goni-,gono-	Greek	reproductive, sexual	gonorrhea, gonad
gymn-, gymno-	Greek	naked, bare	gymnosperm
gyn-, gyne-, gyno-	Greek	woman, female	gynecology
halo-	Greek	salt	halophile
heme-, hemo-	Greek	blood	hemotologist
hemi-	Greek	half	hemisphere
hepta-	Greek	seven	heptane
herb-	Latin	of plants	herbicide
hetero-	Greek	different	heterozygous
hex-, hexa-	Greek	six	hexagonal
hipp-, hippo-	Greek	horse	hippodrome
histo-	Greek	tissue	histamine
holo-	Greek	whole, entire	holistic, hologram
homeo-, homo-	Greek	same, similar	homogeneous
hydr-, hydro-	Greek	pertaining to water	hydrolysis
hyper-	Greek	above, more, over	hyperactive
hypo-	Greek	below, less, under	hypedermic
ichthy-, ichthyo-	Greek	referring to fish	ichthyology
inter-	Latin	between	intercellular
intra-	Latin	within	intracellular
intro-	Latin	inward, within	introvert
iso-	Greek	equal, same	isotonic
kine-	Greek	movement, movement	kinetics
leuc-, leuk-	Greek	white	leucocyte
lycan-	L./Gk.	wolf	lycanthropy
macro-	Greek	large, big, long	macromolecule
man-, manu-	Latin	hand	manual
mastig-	Greek	whip	Mastigophora
meg-, mega-	Greek	great, large	megabyte
melan-, melano-	Greek	black, dark	melanin
mero-	Greek	part, piece	meroblast
mes-, meso-	Greek	middle, in between	Mesozoic
met-, meta-	Greek	later, changed	metamorphosis
micro-	Greek	small	microbiology
milli-	Latin	a thousandth part	millimeter
mio-	Greek	less, smaller	Miocene

PREFIXES	DERIVATIVE	MEANING	EXAMPLE
mito-	Greek	thread	mitosis
mon-, mono-	Greek	one, single	monocular
morph-	Greek	shape, form	morphology
mor-, mort-	Latin	die, death	mortality
muc-, muco-	Latin	many units	multi-cellular
mus-	Latin	mouse, runner	muscle
myco-, mykos-	Greek	fungus, mushroom	mycology
myo-	Greek	muscle	myoglobin
myxo-	Greek	slime, mucus	myxomycetes
nemato-	Greek	thread, threadlike	nematode
neuro-	Greek	sinew, tendon	neurobics
ob-	Latin	against	obtuse
octa-	Greek	eight	octopus
olig-, oligo-	Greek	few, small, less	oligarchy
omni-	Latin	all, everywhere	omnipotent
oo-	Greek	pertaining to an egg	oocyte
ophthalmo-	Greek	referring to the eye	ophthalmologist
opisth-, opistho-	Greek	behind, back	Opisthobranchia
orni-, ornitho-	Greek	bird	ornithology
orth-, ortho-	Greek	straight	orthodontist
osteo-	Greek	bone	osteocyte
oto-	Greek	referring to the ear	otology
ova-, ovi-, ovul-	Latin	egg	ovary, oviduct
paleo-	Greek	old, ancient	paleontology
para-	Greek	beside, near, beyond	parasitism
path-, patho-	Greek	disease, suffer	pathogenic
ped-, pedi-	Latin	foot	pedicure
penna-, pinna-	Latin	feather	pinnate
pent-, penta-	Greek	five	pentagon
per-	Latin	through	pervade, peruse
peri-	Greek	around, surrounding	perimeter
pher-	Greek	bearing, carrying	pheromone
phil-, philo-	Greek	loving, attracted to	philanthropy
phob-	Greek	fear, fearing	phobic
photo-	Greek	pertaining to light	photosynthesis
phyco-	Greek	seaweed, algae	phycology

PREFIXES	DERIVATIVE	MEANING	EXAMPLE
phylo-	Greek	tribe, race, related group	phylogeny
phyto-	Greek	pertaining to plants	phytohormone
plasm-, plasma-	Greek	formative substance	plasmablasts
plati-, platy-	Greek	flat	platypus
pleio-, pleo-	Greek	more, many	pleiomorphic
pod-, poda-, podi-	Greek	foot	podiatrist
poly-	Greek	many	polyhedron
post-	Latin	after	postnatal
pre-	Latin	before	prenatal
preter-	Latin	beyond	preterhuman
prim-	Latin	first	primary
pro-	Greek	before, on behalf of	proboscis
pro-	Latin	forward	progressive
proto-	Greek	first, primary	protozoa
pseudo-	Greek	false	pseudopod
psilo-	Greek	bare, mere	psilopsida
pteri-, ptero-	Greek	fern, feather	pteridophyte
quadr-, quadri-	Latin	four	quadruped
radi-	Latin	ray, spoke of wheel	radial
re-	Latin	back, again	repeat
retro-	Latin	backward	retroactive
rhiz-, rhizo-	Greek	pertaining to roots	rhizoids
rhod-, rhodo-	Greek	a rose, red	rhodopsin
rota-	Latin	wheel	rotate
sarc-, sarco-	Greek	flesh, fleshy	sarcoma
schiz-, schizo-	Greek	split, splitting	schizocoel
se-	Latin	apart	secede
semi-	Latin	half	semicircle
soma-, somato-	Greek	body	somatic
sperma-, spermato-	Greek	seed	spermatozoa
sporo-	Greek	spore	sporophyte
staphylo-	Greek	bunch of grapes	staphylococcus
stoma-	Greek	mouth	stomate
strepto-	Greek	twisted, string of	streptococcus
sub-	Latin	below, under	subapical
supra-, super-	Latin	above, over	supernova

PREFIXES	DERIVATIVE	MEANING	EXAMPLE
sym-, syn-	Greek	together, with	synthesis
taxi-, taxo-	Greek	to make order	taxonomy
tel-, tele-, telo-	Greek	distant, end	telescope
terra-, terre-	Latin	land, earth	terrestial
tetra-	Greek	four	tetrapod
therm-, thermo-	Greek	heat	thermometer
thigmo-	Greek	touch	thigmotaxis
trans-	Latin	across, through	transfer
tri-	Latin	three	triangle
tricho-	Greek	hair	trichocyst
triplo-	Latin	triple	triploid
tropho-	Greek	nourishment	trophoblast
ultra-	Latin	beyond, exceedingly	ultraconservative
uni-	Latin	consisting of one	unicellular
vice-	Latin	in place of	vice-president
vid-, vis-	Latin	see	vision
xen-, xeno-	Greek	alien	xenophobe
zoo-	Greek	animal, life	zoology
zyg-, zygo-	Greek	to join together	zygote

SUFFIXES	DERIVATIVE	MEANING	EXAMPLE
-biosis	Greek	mode of living	symbiosis
-blast	Greek	formative, embryonic	mesoblast
-chaeta, -chete	Greek	a bristle	Polychaeta
-chrome	Greek	color	mercurochrome
-cidal, -cide	Latin	killer, a killing	insecticide
-cocci, -coccus	Greek	round, seed, kernel	streptococcus
-cyst	Greek	pouch, sack	trichocyst
-dactyl	Greek	finger	pentadactyl
-derm, -dermis	Greek	skin, layer	epidermis
-elle, -ule, -let	Latin	small endings	globule, piglet
-emia	Greek	blood disease	anemia

SUFFIXES	DERIVATIVE	MEANING	EXAMPLE
-fer	Latin	bearer, producer, carry	conifer, transfer
-gamy	Greek	marriage, sexual fusion	polygamy
-gen, -geny	Greek	origin, production	progeny, hydrogen
-genesis	Latin	origin, development of	embryogenesis
-graph	Greek	drawing, writing	chromatograph
-hedral, -hedron	Greek	side	polyhedral
-hydrate	Greek	compound formed by union of water with another substance	carbohydrate
-ism	Greek	act, practice or result of	terrorism
-ite	Latin	a division or part	somite
-itis	Greek	inflammation/infection	appendicitis
-jugal, -jugate	Latin	to yoke, join together	conjugate
-logy	Greek	science or study of	biology
-lysis, -lytic	Greek	loosening, separation	photolysis
-mer, -merous	Greek	a part, piece	polymer
-meter	Greek	a measurement	diameter
-morph	Greek	form	endomorph
-mycin	Greek	derived from a fungus	aureomycin
-nomy	Greek	systematized knowledge	astronomy
-oma	Greek	tumorous	carcinoma
-osis, -otic	Greek	abnormal condition	neurosis
-phage	Greek	eater	bacteriophage
-phil, -phile	Greek	having an affinity for	acidophil
-phor, -phore	Greek	bearing, carrying	sporangiophore
-phyll	Greek	leaf	chlorophyll
-phyta, -phyte	Greek	plant	epiphyte
-plasm	Greek	formative substance	cytoplasm
-plast	Greek	organized particle	choroplast
-pod, -poda	Greek	foot	arthropod
-some	Greek	a body	chromosome
-stasis	Greek	a stationary position	homeostasis
-stat, -static	Greek	stationary, still	hemostat
-stomy	Greek	opening into	colostomy
-therm	Greek	heat	homeotherm
-thes, -thesis	Greek	arrangement, in order	hypothesis
-tom, -tomy	Greek	dividing, surgery	lobotomy

SUFFIXES	DERIVATIVE	MEANING	EXAMPLE
-trope, -tropic	Greek	turning	phototropic
-vor, -vore	Latin	feeding	carnivore
-zoa, -zoan, -zoic	Greek	animal, life	protozoa

THE ENTIRE APPENDIX WAS EXTRACTED
FROM ANGELFIRE (N.D.) AND MODIFIED.

APPENDIX B

COMMON LATIN PHRASES

Ad hoc	exactly for that; not prearranged; informal
Ad hominem	(to the man) arguments directed against a person rather than against his arguments
Ad libitum	freely; without restraint; as desired
Ad litem	appointed for a lawsuit
Ad rem	to the point; without digression
Ad valorem	according to its value
Ad infinitum	to infinity
Ad nauseam	to the point of sickness
Alter ego	another; soul mate; close friend
Ars artis gratia	art for the sake of art; art has its own sense
Ars longa vita brevis	art is long, life is short
Agenda	things to be done
Bona fide	in good faith
Carpe diem	literally, sieze the day; enjoy the pleasures of the moment without concern for the future
Casus belli	the occasion or cause for war
Caveat emptor	let the buyer beware
Cogito ergo sum	I think, therefore I am
Compos mentis	of sound mind
Corpus delicti	the body of a sin, or crime; the facts of a crime
Cum laude magnum	with great success

Deus ex machina	lit., God out of a machine; (in ancient Greek and Roman drama) a god introduced into a play to resolve the plot
Dies irae	the day of Wrath
Ecce homo	Behold the man
e pluribus unum	one out of many: the motto of the USA
Et tu, Brute!	And you, Brutus! Spoken by Julius Caesar at his assassination
Exempla gratia	e.g.—for the sake of example
Exeunt	they go out, exit—used as a stage direction
Et alia	et al.—And others
Ergo	therefore
Gloria in excelsis Deo	glory to God in the highest
Habeas corpus	you have (the) body
Id est	i.e.—that is
In absentia	in the absence of
In camera	in chambers (in private)
In extremis	(1) in extremity, in dire straits; (2) at the point of death
In flagrante delicto	while the crime is ablaze; caught in the act.
Infra	(in annotation) below, further on
In loco parentis	in place of a parent:
In medias res	into the midst of things
In perpetuum	for ever
In situ	in the natural, original, or appropriate position
In toto	totally
In utero	within the womb
In vacuo	in isolation; without reference to facts or evidence
In vino veritas	in wine truth
Inter alia	among other things
Inter alios	among other people
Inter se	among or between themselves
Inter vivos	in law, between living people
Ipso facto	by the fact itself
Ipse dixit	an arbitrary and unsupported assertion
Magnum opus	great (large) work
Mea culpa	my fault
Mens sana in corpore sano	a sound mind in a sound body

Morituri te s	
alutamus	we who are about to die salute you
N.B.—Nota Bene	note well
Nec plus ultra	the extreme or perfect point or state [literally: not more beyond; that is, go no further]
Nihil	nothing, nil
Nil Desperandum	never despair
Non licet	it is not permitted
Non compos mentis	not in control of one's own mind
Nolo contendere	I am unwilling to contest
Non sequitur	it does not follow
Pater familias	is head of family, or head of tribe
Pax vobiscum	peace be with you
Persona grata	a welcome person
Persona non grata	an unacceptable or unwelcome person
Per se	by itself
Prima facie	at first view
Pro bono publico	for the public good
Pro Tem (Pro	
Tempera)	for the time being
QED—Quod Est	
Demonstradum	that which has been proven
Quid pro quo	something for something; a reciprocal exchange
Res	a thing, matter, object
RIP Requiescat In	
Pace	may he rest in peace
Semper fidelis	always faithful
Semper paratus	always prepared
Sic	thus
Sic transit gloria	
mundi	thus passes the glory of the world; it is transitory
Sine die	without a day fixed
Sine qua non	without which not; an essential requirement
Sub rosa	under the rose (secretly)
Summum bonum	highest good: the principle of goodness
Tabula rasa	blank slate
Tempus fugit	time flies
Terra incognita	unknown land

Vice versa	turn in place; the other way round
Viz (viclicet)	namely
Veni vidi vici	I came, I saw, I conquered
Vox populi vox	
Dei	the voice of the people is the voice of God

MODIFIED AND EXPANDED
FROM REDBRICK (N.D.)

APPENDIX C

ARTIFACTS

LATIN DECLENSIONS

NOUNS

1st Declension (F.) *puella, -ae*   girl

	CASE	SINGULAR	PLURAL
Subject/complement	Nominative	*puell*a	*puell*ae
Possessive–"of"	Genitive	*puell*ae	*puell*arum
Indirect object–"to/for"	Dative	*puell*ae	*puell*īs
Direct object–"*ad*, to"	Accusative	*puell*am	*puell*ās
Preposition–"*ab*, from"	Ablative	*puell*ā	*puell*īs
A person addressed	Vocative	*puell*a	*puell*ae

2nd Declension (M.) *servus, - ī*   slave

	CASE	SINGULAR	PLURAL
	Nom.	*serv*us	*serv*ī
	Gen.	*serv*ī	*serv*orum
	Dat.	*serv*ō	*serv*īs
	Acc.	*serv*um	*serv*ōs
	Abl.	*serv*ō	*serv*īs
	Voc.	*serv*e	*serv*i

2nd Declension "-r" (M.)   2nd Declension Neuter

ager, -ri   field   *baculum, -a*   stick

CASE	SINGULAR	PLURAL	SINGULAR	PLURAL
Nom.	*ager*	*agr*i	*bacul*um	*bacul*a
Gen.	*agr*ī	*agr*ōrum	*bacul*ī	*bacul*ōrum
Dat.	*agr*ō	*agr*īs	*bacul*ō	*bacul*īs
Acc.	*agr*um	*agr*ōs	*bacul*um	*bacul*a
Abl.	*agr*ō	*agr*īs	*bacul*ō	*bacul*īs
Voc.	*ager*	*agr*ī	*bacul*um	*bacul*a

3rd Declension (M.)

pater, patris father

CASE	SINGULAR	PLURAL
Nom.	*pater*	*patrēs*
Gen.	*patris*	*patrum*
Dat.	*patrī*	*patribus*
Acc.	*patrem*	*patrēs*
Abl.	*patre*	*patribus*
Voc.	*pater*	*patrēs*

3rd Declension (F.)

vox, vocis voice

CASE	SINGULAR	PLURAL
Nom.	*vox*	*vocēs*
Gen.	*vocis*	*vocum*
Dat.	*vocī*	*vocibus*
Acc.	*vocem*	*vocēs*
Abl.	*voce*	*vocibus*
Voc.	*vox*	*vocēs*

LATIN QUIZ STUDY SHEET

1. To find — *invenio, -ire* (invent)
2. Good — *bonus, -a, -um* (bonus)
3. To call together — *convoco, -are* (convocation)
4. To ask — *rogo, -are* (interogative)
5. Vineyard — *vinea, -ae* f. (vineyard)
6. Dog — *canis, -is* m. /f. (canine)
7. To bring, carry — *fero, ferre,* irreg. (ferry)
8. To smell — *olfacio, -ere* (olfactory)
9. With — *cum,* prep +abl. (magna cum laude)
10. Tracks — *vestigia* (vestigial, investigate)
11. Motionless — *immobilis* (immobilize)
12. By the tunic — *tunica* (tunic)
13. To drag — *traho, -ere, tractus* (tractor)
14. Wind — *ventus, -i,* m. (ventilate)
15. Wave — *unda, -ae,* f. (undulate)
16. To escape — *evado, -ere, evasi* (evade, evasion)
17. To grow strong, get well — *convalesco, -ere* (convalesce)
18. Poor — *pauper, pauperis* (pauper)
19. To resist — *resisto, -ere* (resist)
20. To overcome — *supero, -are* (superior, super-)
21. Wound — *vulnus, vulneris,* n. (vulnerable)
22. To bind up — *ligo, -are* (ligature)
23. To trust, believe — *credo, -ere, -idi, -itus* (creed, credible)
24. Carefree, unconcerned — *securus, -a, -um* (secure)
25. Fear — *timor, timoris,* m. (timorous)
26. Affected, overcome — *affectus, -a, -um* (affection)
27. More quickly — *celerius,* adv. (accelerate)
28. Easily — *facile,* adv. (facility)
29. Brave — *fortis, fortis, forte*   (fortify, forte)
30. Greatest — *summus, -a, -um* (summit)
31. Heavy, serious — *gravis, grave* (grave, gravity)
32. To strike — *percutio, -ere; percussus, -i* (percussion)
33. Diligent — *diligens, diligentis* (diligence)

VERBS
1st Conjugation: *parō*, I prepare
parāre, to prepare, *paravi, paratus*

PRESENT

	SINGULAR	PLURAL	
I prepare	*par*ō	*par*āmus	we prepare
you prepare	*par*ās	*par*ātis	you (pl.) prepare
he, she, it prepares	*par*at	*par*ant	they prepare

Imperative

*par*ā!	*par*āte!	prepare!

IMPERFECT

	SINGULAR	PLURAL	
I was preparing	*par*ābam	*par*ābāmus	we were preparing
you were preparing	*par*ābās	*par*ābātis	you (pl.) were preparing
he was preparing	*par*ābat	*par*ābant	they were preparing

PERFECT

	SINGULAR	PLURAL	
I did prepare	*par*āvi	*par*āvimus	we prepared
you prepared	*par*āvisti	*par*āvistis	you (pl.) prepared
he prepared	*par*āvit	*par*āverunt	they prepared

FUTURE

	SINGULAR	PLURAL	
I will prepare	*par*ābō	*par*ābimus	we will prepare
you will prepare	*par*ābis	*par*ābitis	you will prepare
he will prepare	*par*ābit	*par*ābunt	they will prepare

PLUPERFECT

	SINGULAR	PLURAL	
I had prepared	*par*āveram	*par*āverāmus	we had prepared
you had prepared	*par*āverās	*par*āverātis	you had prepared
he had prepared	*par*āverat	*par*āvērant	they had prepared

FUTURE PERFECT

	SINGULAR	PLURAL	
I will have carried	*par*āveram	*par*āverāmus we will have carried
you will have carried	*par*āverās	*par*āverātis you will have carried
he will have carried	*par*āverat	*par*āverānt they will have carried

LATIN I - SAY IT IN LATIN!

Heus!	Hello! (Hi!)
Salvete, discipuli!	Good morning, pupils!
Salve magister!	Good morning, teacher!
Adsum!	Present! (I am here!)
Ubi est Verginia?	Where is Virginia?
Abest; *aegra est.*	She is absent; she is ill.
Ubi est Paulus?	Where is Paul?
Abest; *aeger*	He is absent; he is ill.
Conside/ -ite	Sit down!
Surge/ -ite	Stand up!

Aperite libros!	Open your books!
Claudite libros!	Close your books!
Ponite libros!	Lay aside your books!
Audi/ -ite!	Listen!
Spectal/ -ate!	Look! Watch!
Lege/ -ite Anglice/Latine!	Read in English/Latin
Verte/ -ite Anglice/Latine!	Change to English/Latin
Scribe/ -ite in tabula!	Write on the board!
Sumite chartam et stilos!	Take paper and pencils!
Chartas vestra mihi date!	Give me your papers!
Bene! *Macte*!	Good! Well done!

❧

MR. PAUL
8/20/07
The XYZ SCHOOL

LATIN COURSE REQUIREMENTS
(Please keep this syllabus for future reference)

Expectations:

1. You must bring all necessary books, papers, writing instruments and assignments to class each day. You will not receive any credit for the day on which you are not prepared.

2. All assignments are to be completed, and completed on time: they will form a large part of your grade. Exceptions will require a note from home. Handing in a late assignment will result in a loss of credits.

3. You must do the homework assignments. There is just no way to learn a foreign language without memorization. If you

don't think you can give it a solid half-hour (minimum) per night, you should reconsider taking Latin.

Grading:

1. Quarterly Tests and quizzes will make up 40% of your final grade; the Final Exam counts for 20%.

2. Homework assignments collectively compose 40% of your final grade.

3. You earn credits each day for doing your daily assigned work. Bonus credits can be acquired by active and enthusiastic participation, work thoroughly done or extra credit assignments.

4. If you do not participate in class, credits will be deducted.

Tests & Quizzes

1. Each test or quiz will be announced in advance.

2. If you were present the day before a test or quiz, there will be no excuse for not taking it.

3. Plan Ahead: You must take home your books to study for the test/quiz, even if a weekend or holiday intervenes.

WHAT CAN YOU EXPECT FROM ME?

1. I will never embarrass you in any way.

2. I will never let you hurt each other, physically or verbally.

3. You must feel safe and comfortable in the classroom, no matter how well you achieve, or what questions you may ask.

4. You will always be able to say, "My teacher likes me. I can try,

and not be afraid of failing or being criticized."

5. I will respect you as a person and take as much time with you
as is necessary to help you understand and succeed.

6. If there is anything I don't have an answer for, I will tell you
so. But I am not just putting you off; I will find the answer,
and get back to you.

Remember: *You* must learn Latin. I can only guide your learning. The re-
sponsibility for learning this language is yours. I cannot make you study, or
memorize lists of vocabulary words, verb endings, and declensions. I cannot
help you to choose to do your translation assignments instead of doing other
things at home. I will assume you possess the maturity to be self-motivated.

We will cover the following material this year:

> 1st Quarter: Chapters 1–6
> 2nd Quarter: Chapters 7–13
> 3rd Quarter: Chapters 14–20
> 4th Quarter: Chapters 21–21-27

I will teach all of the above without sacrificing proficiency for expedi-
ency. But if at the end of the 3rd quarter it looks like we will not finish, when
entering the 4th quarter I will teach the necessary subjects, and give all the
vocabulary words with quizzes to so we can complete the book by the end
of the school year.

Methods used to teach:

1. I will assign homework each night: either a translation or a
vocabulary quiz will be required.
2. During class there will be time for discussion of what has been
read the night before. Using questions and a group participation approach, we will learn from each other.
3. Flash cards are necessary for learning vocabulary, and must
be reviewed on a regular, on-going basis to be retained.
4. Videos recreating Roman culture and events in Roman his-

tory will be used occasionally.

5. I hope to have guest speakers from time to time, persons who have visited Roman ruin sites, have slide presentations, displays of artifacts, etc.

6. Original documents such as the *Aeneid*, Caesar's *Gallic Wars* and the Vulgate Latin Bible will be utilized to introduce students to the classics written in Latin.

7. Students will write for purposes of experience, obtaining and conveying information, explaining ideas and opinions, and persuading; they will plan, draft, revise, and edit written material; use correct grammar, sentence structure, vocabulary, spelling, punctuation, and capitalization to convey meaning.

8. Students will be expected to demonstrate knowledge of aspects of Roman culture such as daily life, education, history, geography, government, economics, and the arts.

About the midpoint in the year I will pass out the following list:

SIGN-UP SHEET

A LIST OF POTENTIAL SUBJECTS FOR A BIOGRAPHY:

Aeneas
Alexander the Great
Aristotle
Augustus Caesar
Brutus
Caligula
Cicero
Claudius
Cleopatra
Hadrian
Hannibal
Herod the Great
Homer
Horace
Julius Caesar
Livy

Marc Antony
Marcus Aurelius
Nero
Ovid
Plato
Pliny
Socrates
Tiberius
Titus
Trajan
Virgil

During the third quarter, students will choose three persons (because of inevitable overlaps) and I will assign one person from Greco-Roman History to each student—and that student will become that person. Each Friday there will be two biographies presented as outlined below.

BIOGRAPHY ASSIGNMENT FOR LATIN CLASSES

Requirements

Length: About 5 pages double spaced (should take about 10 minutes to read aloud).

Reports must be written in the first person—example: "My name is Julius Caesar. I was born in . . ."

You will be graded on:

Originality:

Does your report sound like it was copied from an encyclopedia?

Did you include quotes from your subject?

Poems?

Delivery:

>   Enthusiasm. Do you care about this person's life? Do you present that person in such a way as to make the class care about their life?

Application:

>   When done with 'being' the subject, tell how this person has impacted you. Describe how this person has impacted history. What would history have been like if this person had not lived? How did the decisions this person made affect their happiness, and that of those around them?

Extra Credit: Dress up as the person you are portraying.

BIBLIOGRAPHY

Abbot, Martha Gordon. (1991). Critical instructional issues in the classics for American schools. *Foreign Language Annals*. 24(1), 27–37.

Angelfire. (n.d.). Latin-Greek derivatives. Retrieved April 13, 2007 from http://www.angelfire.com/de/nestsite/modbiogreek.html

Barrett, Conrad. (2007). Keys to language and cultural awareness. Retrieved November 8, 2007, from http://www.bolchazy.com/al/keys.html

Baumler, Gary P. (1980). The two track system, its necessity and value. Retrieved March 12, 2007 from http://www.wlsessays.net/subjects/E/esubind.html

Bogdan, Robert C. & Sari Knopp Biklen. (2003). *Qualitative research for education: An introduction to theory and methods*. Boston: Allyn and Bacon.

Burke, Edward P. (1985). Latin for English? A high school case study. Unpublished EdD dissertation, Temple University.

California State Board of Education (2003). Foreign language framework for California public schools. [Electronic version]. Retrieved April 5, 2007, from the CSBOE Web site: http://www.cde.ca.gov/re/pn/fd/ documents/foreign-language.pdf

Chomsky, Noam. (1988), *Language and problems of knowledge: The Managua lectures*, Cambridge, MA: MIT Press.

Clark, Beverly A. (2000). First- and second-language acquisition in early childhood. [Electronic version]. Retrieved March 14, 2007, from ERIC database: http// search.epnet. com/login.aspx?direct=true&db=eric& an=ED47089

Cohen, Arthur M. (1998). *The shaping of American higher education: Emergence and growth of the contemporary system*. San Francisco: Jossey-Bass.

Cook, Vivian. (1993). *Linguistics and second language acquisition: Modern linguistics series*. NY: St. Martins Press.

Creswell, John W. (2005). *Educational research: Planning, conducting, and evaluating quantitative and qualitative research*. Upper Saddle River, NJ: Pearson Merrill Prentice Hall.

D'Souza, Dinesh. (1992). *Illiberal education: The politics of race and sex on campus*. NY: Vintage Books.

De Souza-Wyatt, Betsy-Ann. (2004). A multi-strategy approach to increase ESOL student performance on the high-stakes Virginia end-of-course biology standards of learning (SOL) assessment. [Electronic version]. Retrieved March 12, 2007 from http://64.233.167.104

DeVane, Alice K. (1997). Efficacy of Latin studies in the information age: A paper submitted for PSY 702: Educational Psychology. Valdosta, GA: Valdosta State University. [Electronic version]. Retrieved February 22,

2007 from http://chiron.valdosta.edu/whuitt/files/
Latin.html

Denzin, Norman K. & Yvonna S. Lincoln, Eds. (2005). *The Sage handbook of qualitative research* (3rd ed.). Thousand Oaks, CA: Sage Publications.

District of Columbia Public Schools. (1971). A study of the effect of Latin instruction on English reading skills of sixth grade students in the public schools of the District of Columbia; School Year, 1970–1971. [Electronic version]. Retrieved June 3, 2007 from ERIC, ED060695

Eskenazi, M. (2000, December 11). The new case for Latin. *Time. 156*(24), 61.

Finch, Andrew E. (2005). Task-based language teaching. The postmodern language teacher: The future of task-based teaching. Kyungpook national university. [Electronic version]. Retrieved December 21, 2006 from http://72.14.253.104

Gall, M. D., Joyce P. Gall, & Walter R. Borg. (2003). *Educational research: An introduction* (7th ed.). Boston: Allyn & Bacon.

Ganschow, Leonore & Richard L. Sparks. (1995, February). Effects of direct instruction in Spanish phonology on the native-language skills and foreign-language aptitude of at-risk foreign language learners. *Journal of Learning Disabilities. 28* (2), 107–120.

González, Justo L. (1984). *The story of Christianity: Vol. 1. The early church to the dawn of the reformation.* San Francisco: HarperOne.

Gutek, Gerald L. (2004). *Philosophical and ideological voices in education.* Boston: Allyn & Bacon.

Haag, Ludwig & Elspeth Stern. (2003). In search of benefits of learning Latin. *Journal of Educational Psychology. 95* (1),

174–179.

Harrington-Leuker, Donna. (1992, August). Latin redux. *Executive Educator. 14*(8), 21–25.

Hayford, Jack. (2001). *Handbook of King's College and Seminary*. Van Nuys, CA: King's College Press.

Holmes, C. T. & Keffer, R. L., (1995). A computerized method to teach Latin and Greek root words: effect on verbal SAT scores. [Electronic version]. Retrieved December 31, 2006 from the Journal of Educational Research, Sep/Oct 95, Volume 89, Issue 1, pages 47–51, 4 pages, Item: (9512124954).

Huberman, Michael & Matthew B. Miles. (2002). *The qualitative researcher's companion*. Thousand Oaks, CA: Sage Publications.

Jacobsen, Donna V. (2004). The effect of Latin on English vocabulary acquisition. [Electronic version]. Retrieved December 30, 2006 from http://www.smsd.org/custom/curriculum/actionresearch2004/Jacobsen.pdf.

Johnson, J., William Allan Kritsonis, & David E. Harrington. (2006). National education dilemma: What does a student need to know? Answer? Ways of knowing through the realms of meaning. *National Forum of Teacher Education Journal. 17*(3). ERIC. [Electronic version]. Retrieved December 31, 2006 from http://www.eric.ed.gov/ERICDocs/data/ericdocs2/content_storage_01/0000000b/ 80/33/9c/43.pdf

Jordan, Victoria. (1999). Latin students superior in SAT. The Pennsylvania classical association department of classics, Duquesne university. Spring 2001. [Electronic version]. Retrieved December 31, 2006 from http://scholar.google.com/scholar?hl=en&lr=&safe=off&q=cache:WoKkwgz8tvUJ:www.departments.

bucknell.edu/classics/pca/newsletter_sp2001.
pdf+Latin+%2B%22SAT+scores%22

Kvale, Steinar. (1996). *InterViews: An introduction to qualitative research interviewing.* Thousand Oaks, CA: Sage Publications.

Kennedy, Christoper J. (2006). The study of Latin and its correlation with improved English abilities. Unpublished dissertation for the College of Education of Touro University International.

Kline, Malcolm A. (2006). Academics KO grammar again. [Electronic version]. Campus Report Online.net, retrieved December 31, 2006 from http://www.campus-reportonline.net/ main/articles.php?id=1095

Kurfiss, Joanne G. (1988). Critical thinking: Theory, research, practice, and possibilities. ASHE-ERIC Higher Education Report, No. @. Washington, DC: Association for the Study of Higher Education.

Latin Language Website (2007). [Electronic version]. Retrieved November 15, 2007 from the Latin Language Website: http://www.latinlanguage.org

Levine, Harold G. (1985). Principles of data storage and retrieval for use in qualitative evaluations. *Educational Evaluation and Policy Analysis 7*(2), 169–186.

Lincoln, Yvonna S. & Egon G. Guba. (1985). *Naturalistic inquiry.* Newbury Park, CA: Sage Publications.

Lindzey, Ginny. (2003, November 17). Latin and the GRE. [Electronic version]. Retrieved April 6, 2007 from the NCLG Web site: http://www.promotelatin.org/latin.htm

Lofland, John. (1971). *Analyzing social settings.* Belmont, CA: Wadsworth.

Lucas, Christopher J. (1994). *American higher education: A history.* NY: St. Martin's Press.

Marshall, Catherine & Gretchen B. Rossman. (2006). *Designing qualitative research.* Newbury Park, CA: Sage Publications.

Masciantonio, Rudolph. (1977, September). Tangible benefits of the study of Latin: A review of research. *Foreign Language Annuals. 10*(4), 375–382.

Merriam, Sherran B. (1998). *Qualitative research and case study applications in education.* San Francisco, CA: Jossey-Bass.

Miles, Matthew B. & A. Michael Huberman. (1994). *Qualitative data analysis: An expanded sourcebook.* Thousand Oaks, CA: Sage Publications.

Mishler, Elliot George. (1986). *Research interviewing: Context and narrative.* Cambridge, MA: Harvard University Press.

Morrell, Kenneth Scott. (2006). Language acquisition and teaching ancient Greek: Applying recent theories and technology. In John Gruber-Miller (Ed.), *When dead tongues speak*, 134–157. NY: Oxford University Press.

Ostler, Nicholas. (2007). *Ad infinitum: A biography of Latin.* NY: Walker & Co.

Paul, Richard & Linda Elder. (2004). Universal Intellectual Standards. [Electronic version]. Retrieved December 31, 2006 from the Foundation for Critical Thinking Web site: http://www.criticalthinking.org/resources/articles/universal-intellectual-standards.shtml

Perakyla, Anssi. (2005). Analyzing talk and text. In Norman K. Denzin & Yvonna S. Lincoln (Eds.), *The Sage Handbook of Qualitative Research* (3rd ed.), 869–886. Thousand Oaks, CA: Sage Publications.

Polkinghorne, Donald E. (1991). Two conflicting calls for methodological reform. *Counseling Psychologist*, 19, 103–114.

Potemra, M. (2002). The case for Parnassus. *National Review*. May 20. *54*(9), 57–59.

Prager, Richard. (2000, March). Introductory language: Opening new doors. *Middle School Journal. 20*(3), 178.

Progressive Education Association (1935). Latin in the public schools. *Modern Language Journal. 20*(3), 178.

Redbrick, (n.d.). Melmoth's Latin phrasebook. [Electronic version]. Retrieved May 18, 2007 from http://www.redbrick.dcu.ie/~melmoth/latin.html

Rossman, Mark. (1993). A framework for critical reading. [Electronic version]. Retrieved January 18, 2007 from http://64.233.167.104/search?q=cache:9pH9cRAZl4 8J: www.wilmetteinstitute.us.bahai.org/contents/documents/CRITREED.pdf+mark+rossman+framework+ 1993&hl=en&gl=us&ct =clnk&cd=1

Rubin, Herbert J. & Irene S. Rubin. (1995). *Qualitative interviewing*. Thousand Oaks, CA: Sage Publications.

Ruccolo, Cara. (2004, November). Revisiting a high school classic. *American School Board Journal. 191*(11), 13.

Sayers, Dorothy, L. (1947). The lost tools of learning. [Electronic version].Retrieved March 13, 2007 from http://www.gbt.org/text/sayers.html

Schmidt, Peter. (2007). High school students are aiming higher without improving their performance, federal studies find. *The Chronicle of Higher Education*. [Electronic version]. Retrieved February 23, 2007 from http://chronicle.com/ daily/2007/02/2007022301n.html

Shapiro, S. O. (2007, Summer). Cicero and today's intermediate college-level student. *The Classical Outlook: Journal of*

The American Classical League. 84(4), 147-152.

Shelton, Sue. (2000). Breathing new life into a dead language: Teaching Latin online. (Industry Trend or Event): An article from: *T H E Journal (Technological Horizons In Education)*. [Electronic version]. Retrieved March 12, 2007 from http://www.thejournal.com/articles/14674

Sheridan, Rita. (1976). Augmenting reading skills through language learning transfer. FLES Latin evaluation program evaluation reports, 1973–1974, 1974–1975, 1975–1976. [Electronic version]. Retrieved April 6, 2007 from the Ebsco Web site: http:// search.epnet.com/ login.aspx? direct=true&db=eric&an=ED135218.

Simon, Marilyn K. & J. Bruce Francis. (2001). *The dissertation and research cookbook: From soup to nuts.* Dubuque, IA: Kendall/Hunt.

Sparks, Richard L., Kay Fluharty, Leonore Ganschow, & Sherwin Little. (December 1995–January 1996). An exploratory study on the effects of Latin on the native language skills and foreign language aptitude of students with and without learning disabilities. *The Classical Journal.* 91, 165–184.

Strauss, Anselm M. & Juliet Corbin. (1998). *Basics of qualitative research: Techniques and procedures for developing grounded theory* (3rd ed.). Newbury Park, CA: Sage Publications.

Strauss, Anselm M. & Juliet Corbin. (1994). Grounded theory methodology: and overview. In N. K. Denzin and Y. S. Lincoln (Eds.). *Handbook of qualitative research,* 273–385. Thousand Oaks, CA: Sage Publications.

Teacher Magazine (2007). Classical Education. [Electronic version]. Retrieved August 20, 2007 from http://blogs.edweek.org/teachers/webwatch/2006/11/Classical_educ

ation. html?qs=Classical.

The classical academy. (2006). [Electronic version]. Retrieved February 25, 2007 from http://www.tcad20.org/default.asp

The Scottish group. (1995). *Ecce Romani II-A: A Latin reading program*. Longman, NY: The Scottish Group.

Van Maanen, John. (1988). *Tales of the field: On writing ethnography*. Chicago: University of Chicago Press.

Van Tassel-Baska, Joyce L. (1981). An experimental study of the teaching of Latin to verbally precocious seventh graders. [Electronic version]. Retrieved April 4, 2007 from the Proquest Web site: http://proquest.umi.com/pqdweb? did=749344241&sid=1&Fmt=2&clientId =29440&RQT=309&VName=PQD.

Van Tassel-Baska, Joyce L. (2004, Winter). Quo vadis? Laboring in the classical vineyards: An optimal challenge for gifted secondary students. *The Journal of Secondary Gifted Education. XV*(2), 56–60.

Veith, Gene Edward Jr. (1994). *Postmodern Times, A Christian guide to contemporary thought and culture*. Wheaton, IL: Good News.

Veith, Gene Edward Jr. and Andrew Kern. (2001). *Classical education: The movement sweeping America*. Washington, DC: Capital Research Center.

Walqui, Aida. (2000). Contextual factors in second language acquisition. ERIC Digest [Electronic version]. Retrieved April 7, 2007 from ERIC Web site: http://search.epnet.com/loginaspx?direct=true&db=eric&can= ED444381.

White, Lydia. (1989). *Universal grammar and second language acquisition*, Amsterdam, the Netherlands: John Benjamins.

Wiley, Patricia D. (1984). High school foreign language study
    and college academic performance. *Classical Outlook*.
    62(2). 33–36.

Wiley, Patricia D. (1989, November). The impact of high school
    foreign language study on academic success in college:
    A 1989 research update. Paper presented at the Annual
    Meeting of the Mid-South Education Research Asso-
    ciation (Little Rock, AR, November 9, 1989).

Young-Scholten, Martha. (1999). Focus on form and linguistic
    competence: Why Krashen is still right about acquisi-
    tion. [Electronic version]. Retrieved December 31,
    2006 from ERIC, ED432919, Capella Library.

Jeffry L. Smith, BA, MAT, PhD is a profes[sor] at The King's University, where he taught Theology, Church History, and N[ew] Testament Greek. Dr. Smith has been a Ch[ris]tian for nearly half a century, coming to the L[ord] in 1962. Originally from Southern California[,] and his wife of 32 years, RaNae, currently m[ake] their home in Southern Colorado.

American education commonly struggles with a gap between scholarly research a[nd] classroom application. With specialized academic research on one side and en[tre]preneurial self-help on the other, educators sometimes find themselves trying [to] leap across the chasm, while many parents try to guide their children onto solid ground[.] *The Lost Tools of Learning* Jeffry Smith provides a sterling example of a practical way [to] bridge the gap.

Increasing educational emphasis on student performance on standardized tests has gi[ven] rise to a new and costly industry: test coaching for college admission, especially the hig[hly] visible Scholastic Aptitude Test (SAT). *The Lost Tools of Learning* describes an "old-n[ew]" alternative that can provide a better way. In addition to his own qualitative research, [Dr.] Smith analyzed in his dissertation a number of studies showing that the learning of cla[ssi]cal languages, especially Latin, teaches children and adolescents a disciplined way to le[arn.] Classical language learning carries over into other subjects and improves test performa[nce.] So, instead of being framed as forcing students to learn irrelevant "dead" languages, stu[dy]ing Latin and Greek teaches young people to learn in new ways.

This well-documented book reminds both parents and educators that the retrieva[l of] wisdom from past educational practices offers one way to negotiate the challenges of [the] future. As the Latin proverb declares, "*Non nova sed nove*. Not new things but in a n[ew] way."

— Charles J. Scalise
Professor of Church History
Fuller Theological Seminary

$16.9[9]

Parson's Porch Books
Cleveland, TN

Parson's Porch Books
Cleveland, Tennessee
www.parsonsporchbooks.com

ISBN 978-1-936912-24[-7]
516[?]

9 781936 912247

www.ingramcontent.com/pod-product-compliance
Lightning Source LLC
Chambersburg PA
CBHW021111090426
42738CB00006B/593